REFLECT
LISTENING & SPEAKING

LAURIE BLASS

MARI VARGO

NATIONAL GEOGRAPHIC
LEARNING

Australia · Brazil · Mexico · Singapore · United Kingdom · United States

National Geographic Learning,
a Cengage Company

Reflect 3 Listening & Speaking
Authors: Laurie Blass & Mari Vargo

Publisher: Sherrise Roehr
Executive Editor: Laura Le Dréan
Senior Development Editor: Eve Einselen Yu
Director of Global Marketing: Ian Martin
Product Marketing Manager: Tracy Baillie
Senior Content Project Manager: Mark Rzeszutek
Media Researcher: Eileen Sweeney
Art Director: Brenda Carmichael
Senior Designer: Lisa Trager
Operations Coordinator: Hayley Chwazik-Gee
Manufacturing Buyer: Mary Beth Hennebury
Composition: MPS Limited

Student Book ISBN: 978-0-357-44913-4
Student Book with Online Practice: 978-0-357-44919-6

National Geographic Learning
200 Pier 4 Boulevard
Boston, MA 02210

Locate your local office at **international.cengage.com/region**

Visit National Geographic Learning online at **ELTNGL.com**
Visit our corporate website at **www.cengage.com**

Printed in China
Print Number: 01   Print Year: 2021

SCOPE AND SEQUENCE

SPEAKING & PRONUNCIATION	GRAMMAR	CRITICAL THINKING	REFLECT ACTIVITIES
Give a presentation Word stress	Verbs + gerunds or infinitives	Brainstorm solutions	▶ Consider where people meet in a big city ▶ Evaluate activities that bring people together ▶ Brainstorm ways to meet your neighbors ▶ **UNIT TASK** Present a plan to help people connect
Take turns in a discussion Stress in words with suffixes	Future real conditionals	Support your opinions	▶ Give your opinion about learning a language ▶ Explain the effect of learning a second language ▶ Discuss how language and culture are related ▶ **UNIT TASK** Present a saying or proverb
Ask for and give clarification Rhythm and stress: content vs. structure words	Simple past and past continuous	Evaluate data	▶ Discuss the issue of fake news ▶ Consider how to deal with fake news ▶ Interpret an infographic about fake news ▶ **UNIT TASK** Evaluate and present a news story
Define and explain specific terms Reduced structure words	Connecting words for reasons and results	Analyze motivations	▶ Evaluate street art ▶ Analyze the motivations of artists ▶ Discuss art careers ▶ **UNIT TASK** Give a presentation about a work of art

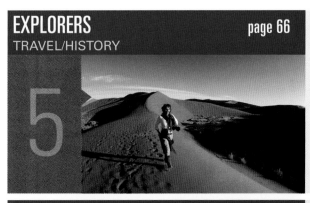

SPEAKING & PRONUNCIATION	GRAMMAR	CRITICAL THINKING	REFLECT ACTIVITIES
Ask follow-up questions Final intonation	Present perfect	Preview a listening	▶ Discuss what it means to be an explorer ▶ Consider explorers, past and present ▶ Discuss exploration, past and present ▶ **UNIT TASK** Role-play an interview with an explorer
Present arguments for and against Focus words	Unreal present and future conditional	Categorize ideas	▶ Discuss how our memories affect our behavior ▶ Relate ideas about memory to your life ▶ Consider reasons for removing a memory ▶ **UNIT TASK** Debate ideas about changing memories
Present results Connected speech	-ing forms	Question ideas	▶ Discuss how boredom and creativity are related ▶ Question ideas about boredom ▶ Evaluate how personal habits affect creativity ▶ **UNIT TASK** Present the results of a challenge to be more creative
Use signal words and phrases Thought groups	Infinitives of purpose	Evaluate pros and cons	▶ Consider reasons for joining a club or team ▶ Evaluate your attitude toward video gaming ▶ Discuss players and types of video games ▶ **UNIT TASK** Present a review of a video game or an app

CONNECT TO IDEAS

Reflect Listening & Speaking features relevant, global content to engage students while helping them acquire the academic language and skills they need. Specially-designed activities give students the opportunity to reflect on and connect ideas and language to their academic, work, and personal lives.

National Geographic photography and content invite students to investigate the world and discuss high-interest topics.

Watch & Speak and **Listen & Speak** sections center on high-interest video and audio that students will want to talk about as they build academic listening and speaking skills.

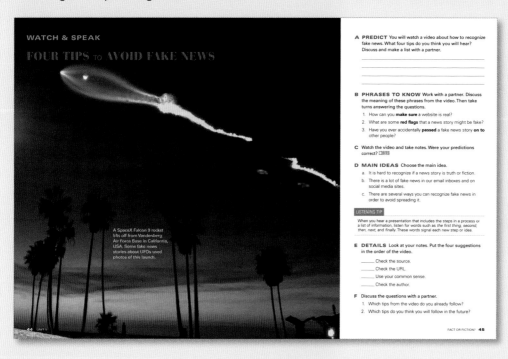

CONNECT TO ACADEMIC SKILLS

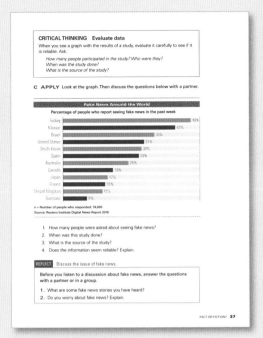

Scaffolded activities build confidence and provide students with a clear path to achieving final outcomes.

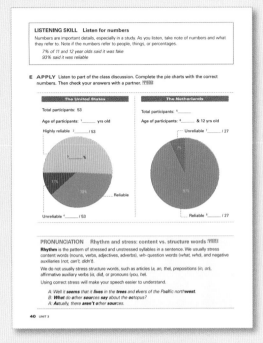

Reflect activities give students the opportunity to think critically about what they are learning and check their understanding.

Focused academic **listening** and **speaking skills** help students communicate with confidence.

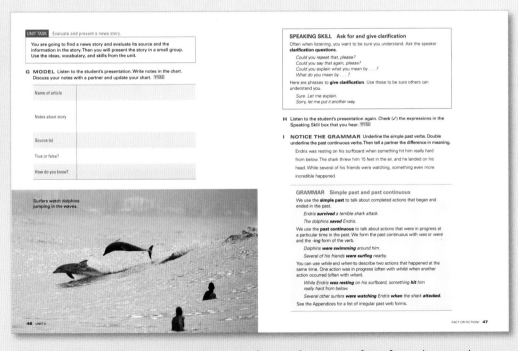

Clear models, relevant grammar, and step-by-step planning give students the support they need to complete the final speaking task successfully.

CONNECT TO ACHIEVEMENT

Reflect at the end of the unit is an opportunity for formative assessment. Students review the skills and vocabulary they have gained.

DIGITAL RESOURCES

TEACH lively, engaging lessons that get students speaking. The Classroom Presentation Tool helps teachers to present the Student's Book pages, play audio and video, and increase participation by providing a central focus for the class.

LEARN AND TRACK with Online Practice and Student's eBook. For students, the mobile-friendly platform optimizes learning through customized re-teaching and adaptive practice. For instructors, progress-tracking is made easy through the shared gradebook.

ASSESS learner performance and progress with the ExamView® Assessment Suite available online.

ACKNOWLEDGMENTS

The Authors and Publisher would like to acknowledge the teachers around the world who participated in the development of *Reflect*.

A special thanks to our Advisory Board for their valuable input during the development of this series.

ADVISORY BOARD

Dr. Mansoor S. Almalki, Taif University, Saudi Arabia; **John Duplice**, Sophia University, Japan; **Heba Elhadary**, Gulf University for Science and Technology, Kuwait; **Hind Elyas**, Niagara College, Saudi Arabia; **Cheryl House**, ILSC Education Group, Canada; **Xiao Luo**, BFUS International, China; **Daniel L. Paller,** Kinjo Gakuin University, Japan; **Ray Purdy**, ELS Education Services, USA; **Sarah Symes,** Cambridge Street Upper School, USA.

GLOBAL REVIEWERS

ASIA

Michael Crawford, Dokkyo University, Japan; **Ronnie Hill**, RMIT University Vietnam, Vietnam; **Aaron Nurse**, Golden Path Academics, Vietnam; **Simon Park**, Zushi Kaisei, Japan; **Aunchana Punnarungsee**, Majeo University, Thailand.

LATIN AMERICA AND THE CARIBBEAN

Leandro Aguiar, inFlux, Brazil; **Sonia Albertazzi-Osorio**, Costa Rica Institute of Technology, Costa Rica; **Auricea Bacelar**, Top Seven Idiomas, Brazil; **Natalia Benavides**, Universidad de Los Andes, Colombia; **James Bonilla**, Global Language Training UK, Colombia; **Diego Bruekers Deschamp**, Inglês Express, Brazil; **Josiane da Rosa**, Hello Idiomas, Brazil; **Marcos de Campos Bueno**, It's Cool International, Brazil; **Sophia De Carvalho**, Ingles Express, Brazil; **André Luiz dos Santos**, IFG, Brazil; **Oscar Gomez-Delgado**, Universidad de los Andes, Colombia; **Ruth Elizabeth Hibas**, Inglês Express, Brazil; **Rebecca Ashley Hibas**, Inglês Express, Brazil; **Cecibel Juliao**, UDELAS University, Panama; **Rosa Awilda López Fernández**, School of Languages UNAPEC University, Dominican Republic; **Isabella Magalhães**, Fluent English Pouso Alegre, Brazil; **Gabrielle Marchetti**, Teacher's House, Brazil; **Sabine Mary**, INTEC, Dominican Republic; **Miryam Morron**, Corporación Universitaria Americana, Colombia; **Mary Ruth Popov**, Ingles Express, Ltda., Brazil; **Leticia Rodrigues Resende**, Brazil; **Margaret Simons**, English Center, Brazil.

MIDDLE EAST

Abubaker Alhitty, University of Bahrain, Bahrain; **Jawaria Iqbal**, Saudi Arabia; **Rana Khan**, Algonquin College, Kuwait; **Mick King**, Community College of Qatar, Qatar; **Seema Jaisimha Terry**, German University of Technology, Oman.

USA AND CANADA

Thomas Becskehazy, Arizona State University, AZ; **Robert Bushong**, University of Delaware, DE; **Ashley Fifer**, Nassau Community College, NY; **Sarah Arva Grosik**, University of Pennsylvania, PA; **Carolyn Ho**, Lone Star College-CyFair, TX; **Zachary Johnsrud**, Norquest College, Canada; **Caitlin King**, IUPUI, IN; **Andrea Murau Haraway**, Global Launch / Arizona State University, AZ; **Bobbi Plante**, Manitoba Institute of Trades and Technology, Canada; **Michael Schwartz**, St. Cloud State University, MN; **Pamela Smart-Smith**, Virginia Tech, VA; **Kelly Smith**, English Language Institute, UCSD Extension, CA; **Karen Vallejo**, University of California, CA.

CREATING
CONNECTIONS

Guisepi Spadafora travels around in his bus offering tea to people. He wants people to meet and form relationships. "I'd like to live in a more sharing world," he says. Brooklyn, USA

IN THIS UNIT

- ► Consider where people meet in a big city
- ► Evaluate activities that bring people together
- ► Brainstorm ways to meet your neighbors
- ► Present a plan to help people connect

SKILLS

LISTENING
Listen for main ideas and details

SPEAKING
Give a presentation

GRAMMAR
Verbs + gerunds or infinitives

CRITICAL THINKING
Brainstorm solutions

CONNECT TO THE TOPIC

1. How does the man in the photo help people to connect? What do you think of this idea?

2. How do people in your community connect with each other?

3

PREPARE TO WATCH

A VOCABULARY Listen to the words. Complete the sentences with the correct form of the words. Use a dictionary if necessary. 🔊 1.1

atmosphere (n)	discover (v)	opportunity (n)	stable (adj)	unique (adj)
average (adj)	obligation (n)	population (n)	trust (v)	whenever (conj)

1. _____ people come to Mountain Lake Park, they always find something fun to do.

2. This neighborhood is very _____. Not much has changed in the last 20 years.

3. Combining a movie theater with a cafe was a(n) _____ idea. I've never seen it before.

4. Over 12 million people live in São Paulo. It has the second largest _____ in Brazil.

5. Vancouver has a nice _____. It's not too crowded, and people are friendly.

6. It's important to have friends you can _____, who are there when you need them.

7. The people in my neighborhood have _____ incomes—not too high and not too low.

8. We _____ a new restaurant down the street. Now we eat there every weekend.

9. If you borrow money, you have a(n) _____ to pay it back. It's the right thing to do.

10. His new job is a great _____. It gives him the chance to learn new skills.

B Listen to the conversation between Eun and Miguel. Complete the chart. Then compare the two cities with a partner. 🔊 1.2

City, Country	Population	Favorite neighborhood	Atmosphere	Unique feature
Seoul, _____	_____ million	Gangnam	_____	Samneung _____
Puebla, _____	_____ million	Centro Histórico	_____	Alley of the _____

C PERSONALIZE Discuss the questions with a partner.

1. Is the **population** of your city or town larger or smaller than the cities in activity B?

2. Describe the **atmosphere** of your neighborhood. Is it noisy or quiet? Friendly or unfriendly?

3. What places or things are **unique** in your neighborhood, town, or city?

D ANALYZE Look at the infographic. Then complete the facts below.

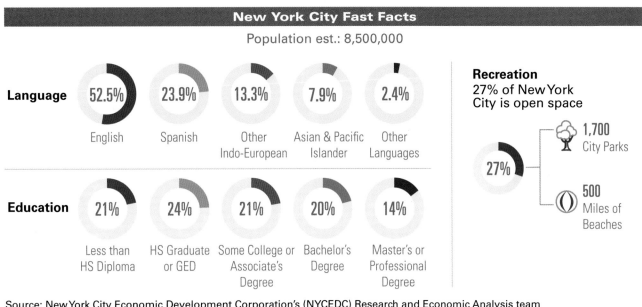

Source: New York City Economic Development Corporation's (NYCEDC) Research and Economic Analysis team

1. Almost one quarter (¼) of New Yorkers speak _____. Just over half speak

   _____.

2. _____ percent of New Yorkers have a bachelor's degree or higher degree.

3. More than one quarter of the space in New York City is _____ space with

   _____ city parks and 500 miles of _____.

REFLECT Consider where people meet in a big city.

You are going to watch a video about a place in New York City where people get together. Discuss the questions in a small group.

1. Where is it easiest to meet people in a big city?

2. Why is it sometimes hard to make friends in a big city?

3. Based on the infographic, what do you think people do for fun in New York City? Where can they go to connect with others?

THE TABLES

Ping-Pong players in
Bryant Park, New York
City, USA

A PREVIEW Answer the questions.

1. What are the people in the photo doing? _____

2. Based on the title and photo, what do you think the video is about? _____

_____

B PHRASES TO KNOW Work with a partner. Discuss the meaning of these phrases from the video. Then take turns answering the questions.

1. Who is **the rock** of your family, your friends, or some other group?

2. In what kinds of jobs can you **make six figures**?

3. Is there a person or a thing (e.g., song, movie) that helps you **get through tough times**?

C MAIN IDEAS Watch the video and choose the three main ideas. ▶1.1

a. The Ping-Pong tables in Bryant Park interest different types of people.

b. Bryant Park provides a comfortable place for homeless people to spend their days.

c. Even though they are very different, the Bryant Park players have created a community.

d. Bryant Park has become the most important place for professional Ping-Pong players to practice.

e. Playing Ping-Pong in Bryant Park has improved some people's lives.

D DETAILS Read the statements. Then watch the video again. Write T for *True*, F for *False*, or NG for *Not Given*. ▶1.1

1. _____ Gregory had a very difficult childhood.

2. _____ Gregory recently learned to play Ping-Pong.

3. _____ The other players have a very positive opinion of Gregory.

4. _____ You have to pay to play Ping-Pong in Bryant Park.

5. _____ You sometimes have to wait a long time to play Ping-Pong in Bryant Park.

6. _____ Rich and poor people play Ping-Pong together in Bryant Park.

7. _____ A student named Gideon helped improve Gregory's life.

8. _____ Another player found Gregory a place to live.

COMMUNICATION TIP

You can give your **opinion** with phrases like:
I (don't) think (that) . . .
In my opinion, . . .

A: **I don't think that** your idea will work.
B: Really? Why? **In my opinion**, it's a great idea.

E DISCUSS Work in a group. Answer the questions. Use phrases for giving opinions.

1. Why are the Ping-Pong tables so successful in Bryant Park?

2. Would Ping-Pong tables work in your community? Explain.

F NOTICE THE GRAMMAR Underline the verbs *hope*, *need*, *plan on*, and *propose*. What forms are the words after these verbs (e.g., noun, verb)? Discuss with a partner. Then take turns completing the statements with your own ideas.

1. I hope to become a/an . . .

2. My town needs to build a/an

3. I plan on going to . . . one day.

4. I propose building a/an . . . near this school.

GRAMMAR Verbs + gerunds or infinitives

A **gerund** is a verb + *-ing* used as a noun. An **infinitive** is *to* + verb. Some verbs are followed only by gerunds. Others are followed only by infinitives.

▸ **Verbs followed by gerunds**: *propose, plan on*

  We **propose putting** *Ping-Pong tables in Central Park.*

▸ **Verbs followed by infinitives**: *expect, hope, need, plan, want*

  The city's leaders **want to build** *a community center in my neighborhood.*

  They don't **expect to pay** *money to play Ping-Pong.*

Note that a gerund follows a preposition. Prepositions are words like *in, on, at, under*.

  She didn't **plan on moving to** *New York, but her company sent her there.*

G GRAMMAR Read the conversation. Choose the correct verb.

A: What are you planning on ¹**to do / doing** this summer?

B: I'm really out of shape, so I hope ²**to get / getting** more exercise.

A: Well, I'm going to learn how to play tennis. Do you want ³**to join / joining** me?
   The neighborhood community center is planning on ⁴**to give / giving** lessons
   this summer. They're not expensive.

B: That sounds like a good idea. But do you need ⁵**to bring / bringing** your own tennis racket?

A: No, the community center has some. I plan ⁶**to borrow / borrowing** one.

B: OK! Let's do this!

A man getting
a tennis lesson

H GRAMMAR Complete the sentences with the gerund or infinitive of the verbs in parentheses.

1. Jack wanted _____ (teach) people to play basketball, so he started an online class.

2. I hope _____ (learn) how to play Ping-Pong someday.

3. My town doesn't plan on _____ (build) any new playgrounds.

4. The gym teacher proposed _____ (organize) soccer teams for the younger students.

5. The parents didn't expect _____ (pay) for their children's soccer uniforms.

6. We need _____ (get) kids from all over the city to play on the teams.

7. The college proposed _____ (put) a basketball court on campus.

8. The city hopes _____ (bring) people from all walks of life to the new sports center.

9. I didn't plan on _____ (see) my neighbor at the park, but she was there.

10. We wanted _____ (play) Ping-Pong, but there were no free tables.

I GRAMMAR Write six questions in your notebook about future plans with these verbs. Take turns asking and answering the questions with a partner.

plan on + do	want + learn	hope + see
plan + play	expect + go	need + study

A: *What do you **plan on doing** this summer?*

B: *I **plan on playing** a new sport.*

REFLECT Evaluate activities that bring people together.

Take turns answering the questions with a partner.

1. Do you do any activities with groups of people? If so, which ones?
2. In your opinion, which games, sports, or activities are the best for bringing people together?

PREPARE TO LISTEN

A VOCABULARY Listen to the words. Then read their definitions and complete the sentences with the correct form of the words. Two words are not used 🎧 **1.3**

actual: (adj) real
appear: (v) to be present for the first time
donation: (n) money or other gift to help a person or place
event: (n) an organized happening, such as a concert
generous: (adj) more than the usual amount

impossible: (adj) not able to happen
issue: (n) a problem
participate: (v) to take part in (an activity)
positive: (adj) good and helpful
support: (n) help and kindness

1. When a large object _____ in downtown Chicago, many thought it looked like a giant bean.

2. This sculpture has had a(n) _____ effect on this area of Chicago. People enjoy gathering around it.

3. Many people call it "The Bean," but its _____ name is Cloud Gate.

4. Weddings and other _____ are sometimes held around the sculpture.

5. When looking at the plan for Cloud Gate, many experts said it would be _____ to build.

6. There were several _____ during the building of Cloud Gate, so it cost more than people thought it would.

7. Cloud Gate cost over 20 million dollars. All the money came from _____ . The city didn't pay for it.

8. My class _____ in a dance festival near Cloud Gate. We learned traditional dances.

The sculpture Cloud Gate in Millennium Park in Chicago, Illinois, USA

B PERSONALIZE Discuss the questions with a partner.

1. What are some important **issues** in your school, city, town, or neighborhood?

2. What neighborhood, school, or city **events** have you **participated** in?

C Look at the infographic. It shows the results of a survey. Then discuss the questions below with a partner.

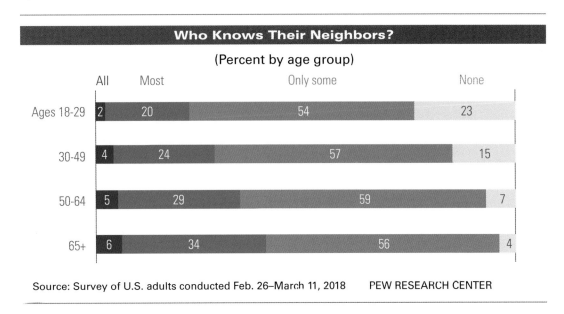

Who Knows Their Neighbors?

(Percent by age group)

	All	Most	Only some	None
Ages 18-29	2	20	54	23
30-49	4	24	57	15
50-64	5	29	59	7
65+	6	34	56	4

Source: Survey of U.S. adults conducted Feb. 26–March 11, 2018   PEW RESEARCH CENTER

1. Where do the participants in the survey live? When was the survey taken?

2. Which age group knows the most neighbors? The fewest? What are possible reasons for these results?

3. Do you think this information is true for your home country? Explain.

CRITICAL THINKING Brainstorm solutions

Brainstorming means thinking of as many ideas as possible and writing them all down. Don't worry about whether your ideas are good or bad *while* you're brainstorming. You can delete or change them later.

COMMUNICATION TIP

We use *could* to make suggestions.

You **could organize** a neighborhood party.

You **could consider** starting a neighborhood sports team.

REFLECT   Brainstorm ways to meet your neighbors.

Work in a small group. Discuss answers to the questions.

1. How many of your neighbors do you know? How did you meet them?

2. Brainstorm ways to meet your neighbors.

Children playing
a street piano in
London, England, UK

CREATIVE WAYS TO CONNECT

A PREVIEW Answer the questions.

1. What are the children in the photo doing? Where are they?
2. Would you play a piano on the street?

LISTENING SKILL   Listen for main ideas and details

When you hear a presentation or lecture, listen for the main ideas and important details. This will help you understand and remember key information.

Main ideas are the most important ideas. Speakers often state the main ideas at the beginning of their presentations. They also often repeat the main ideas at the end.

   The Ping-Pong tables in Bryant Park, New York City, bring people from all walks of life together.

Details support the main ideas. Details can include facts, examples, reasons, and explanations.

   There are several Ping-Pong tables in Bryant Park. (fact)
   A student and a homeless man became friends playing Ping-Pong. (example)

B MAIN IDEAS Listen to the podcast. Choose the correct answer. 🎧 1.4

The podcast is about projects in public spaces that _____.

a. solve neighborhood issues like crime

b. help people connect with each other

c. teach people to appreciate music

C DETAILS Listen again. Complete the chart with details. 🎧 1.4

Ideas	Who thought of it	Why they did it	The result
1 _____ in Bryant Park	Wally Green (a professional Ping-Pong player)	To get more people to 2 _____	People from all walks of life 3 _____.
4 _____ on streets and in other public places	Luke Jerram (an 5 _____)	To bring people together	People play them and 6 _____.
Collaborative 7 _____ in neighborhoods	The Eden Project (an 8 _____)	To get people together and make communities 9 _____	People make new 10 _____ and discuss neighborhood issues.

A skateboard park in Odori
Park, Sapporo, Japan

Present a plan to help people connect.

You are going to present a plan to help people in your community connect with each other.
You will take turns explaining your plan. Use the ideas, vocabulary, and skills from the unit.

D MODEL Listen to a group propose a plan for a skateboard park. Complete the chart. Discuss
your answers with a partner and update your chart. 🎧 1.5

	Plan to help people connect: Build a skateboard park
Reasons	1. _____ 2. _____ 3. _____
Benefits	1. _____ 2. _____ 3. _____

PRONUNCIATION   Word stress 🔊 1.6

In words with two syllables, we usually stress just one syllable. We pronounce the vowel in the stressed syllable more clearly and loudly than the vowel in the other syllable. We often pronounce the unstressed syllable as a schwa (/ə/).

e-**vent**	sup-**port**
/ə/	/ə/

In words with more than two syllables, one syllable has the primary stress, or main stress. We often pronounce unstressed syllables as a schwa (/ə/).

po-pu-**la**-tion	con-**nec**-tion
/ə/ /ə/	/ə/ /ə/

E PRONUNCIATION Read the words with a partner. Guess the stressed syllable in each word and underline it. Then listen and check your answers. 🔊 1.7

1. be-ne-fit   6. po-si-tive

2. pro-pose   7. ac-tu-al

3. ap-pear   8. o-bli-ga-tion

4. par-ti-ci-pate   9. ge-ne-rous

5. phy-si-cal   10. di-sco-ver

F PRONUNCIATION Complete the sentences with words from activity E. Then listen and check your answers. 🔊 1.8

1. We have an _____ to improve our community.

2. I _____ building a skateboard park.

3. There are _____ and social _____ of having a skateboard park for kids.

4. The new swimming pool is free for residents thanks to _____ donations from local businesses.

5. The team _____ a great site for the new farmer's market.

6. Having a group lunch with neighbors had many _____ results, such as a greater feeling of safety and security among residents.

7. The _____ name of the game is table tennis, but many people call it Ping-Pong.

8. We will _____ in the town meeting about the new park.

G PLAN Work in groups. Use the chart to plan your presentation. Then practice your presentation.

	Plan to help people connect:
Reasons	1. _____ 2. _____ 3. _____
Benefits	1. _____ 2. _____ 3. _____

H UNIT TASK Present your plan to the class. As you listen to other groups present, take notes in the chart. Which group has the most interesting plan?

	Plan for Group 1:	Plan for Group 2:
Reasons	1. _____ 2. _____ 3. _____	1. _____ 2. _____ 3. _____
Benefits	1. _____ 2. _____ 3. _____	1. _____ 2. _____ 3. _____

REFLECT

A Check (✓) the Reflect activities you can do and the academic skills you can use.

☐ consider where people meet in a big city   ☐ listen for main ideas and details

☐ evaluate activities that bring people together   ☐ give a presentation

☐ brainstorm ways to meet your neighbors   ☐ verbs + gerunds or infinitives

☐ present a plan to help people connect   ☐ brainstorm solutions

B Write the vocabulary words from the unit in the correct column. Add any other words that you learned. Circle words you still need to practice.

NOUN	VERB	ADJECTIVE	ADVERB & OTHER

C Reflect on the ideas in the unit as you answer these questions.

1. Do you want to be more involved in your community? Explain.

_____

_____

_____

2. What ideas or skills in this unit will be most useful to you in the future?

_____

_____

_____

LANGUAGE AND CULTURE

Men sitting, relaxing, and talking in Abha, Saudi Arabia

IN THIS UNIT

▸ Give your opinion about learning a language

▸ Explain the effect of learning a second language

▸ Discuss how language and culture are related

▸ Present a saying or proverb

SKILLS

LISTENING
Listen for signal words

SPEAKING
Take turns in a discussion

GRAMMAR
Future real conditionals

CRITICAL THINKING
Support your opinions

CONNECT TO THE TOPIC

1. What do you think the men are talking about?

2. How does your culture affect the way you speak?

PREPARE TO LISTEN

A VOCABULARY Listen to the words. Complete the sentences with the correct form of the words. Use a dictionary if necessary. 2.1

according to (prep)	author (n)	field (n)	misunderstanding (n)	speech (n)
attention (n)	background (n)	mention (v)	patient (adj)	widespread (adj)

1. You can say "Excuse me" to get someone's _____.

2. Our professor is the _____ of a book about language and culture. She wrote it a couple years ago.

3. In the southern United States, people pronounce certain words differently than in the north. This is just one example of how _____ differs across the country.

4. Jin's _____ in computers helped him get a job in IT. He has a degree and several years of experience.

5. My classmate didn't _____ that she spoke four languages. I found out later that she speaks Chinese, Spanish, Russian, and English.

6. The use of Spanish is _____ in the United States. Many government documents are in both English and Spanish.

7. I'm really sorry about the _____. I didn't listen to you very carefully. I thought you said that *no one* was sitting in this seat.

8. Carmen finished nursing school and is now working in the medical _____.

9. _____ our English teacher, many Americans do not speak a second language.

10. You need to be _____ to learn another language. It takes time to become fluent.

B PERSONALIZE Discuss the questions with a partner.

1. What **field** of study are you most interested in?

2. When you say something and a person believes you said something else, how can you correct the **misunderstanding**?

3. Are you **patient** with people who don't speak your language well? Give an example.

4. What **authors** do you like? What types of books do they write?

C Look at the chart. Then answer the questions below. Discuss your answers with a partner.

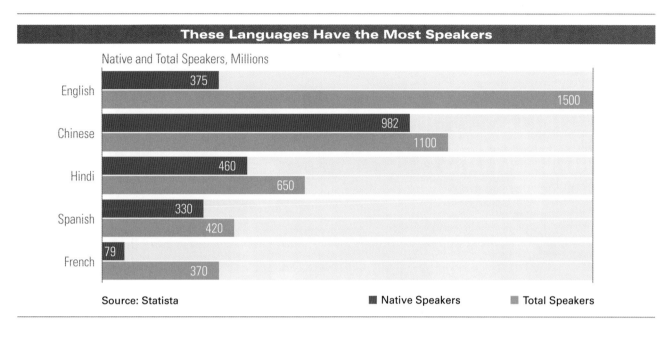

These Languages Have the Most Speakers

Native and Total Speakers, Millions

- English: 375 (Native), 1500 (Total)
- Chinese: 982 (Native), 1100 (Total)
- Hindi: 460 (Native), 650 (Total)
- Spanish: 330 (Native), 420 (Total)
- French: 79 (Native), 370 (Total)

Source: Statista   ■ Native Speakers   ■ Total Speakers

1. Which language has the most native speakers? _____ The most total speakers?

   _____

2. Which two languages have more non-native speakers than native speakers?

   _____ and _____

3. What surprises you about this chart? _____

   _____

CRITICAL THINKING   Support your opinions

When you give your opinion, always give at least one reason to support it. Personal experience and research are both good ways to support your opinions.

I agree that English is the most important second language to learn. People all over the world use English to communicate. Also, more people speak English than any other language.

REFLECT   Give your opinion about learning a language.

You are going to listen to a radio talk show about native and non-native English speakers. Rank the statements by how strongly you agree. Then share your answers with a partner.

1 = strongly agree   2 = agree   3 = disagree   4 = strongly disagree

_____ English is the most important second language to learn.
_____ English speakers do not need to learn a second language.
_____ People who speak two or more languages are more interesting than people who only speak one language.

THE WORLD'S WORST COMMUNICATORS?

An audience listens to a native English speaker at the National Convention Center in Hanoi, Vietnam.

A PREDICT Who do you think the title refers to? Discuss your ideas with a partner. Then listen to an excerpt from a radio show and check your prediction. 🎧 2.2

B PHRASES TO KNOW Work with a partner. Discuss the meaning of the phrases from the radio show. Then take turns answering the questions.

1. When you are talking with someone and they say, "Sorry but **you've lost me**," what should you do?

2. Has an experience ever **opened your eyes** to something new? If so, what happened?

C MAIN IDEAS Listen to the radio show and choose the main idea. 🎧 2.3

a. Most native English speakers don't speak a second language, so they don't always communicate well with non-native English speakers.

b. Native English speakers don't usually change their speech to make it easier for non-native speakers to understand.

c. Non-native English speakers can't understand native speakers well because native speakers use only simple language.

LISTENING SKILL   Listen for signal words

Pay attention to words and phrases that introduce reasons (*because, since*) and results (*so, as a result, that's why*). When you hear one of these words or phrases, you know that what follows is a reason or a result.

Reasons	Results
Because he used a lot of slang, **Since** he used a lot of slang,	we didn't understand him.
He used a lot of slang	**so** we didn't understand him.
He used a lot of slang.	**As a result**, we didn't understand him. **That's why** we didn't understand him.

D APPLY Listen to the excerpts. Complete the chart with the reasons and results. 🎧 2.4

Reasons	Results
1. Native English speakers are not good communicators	
2.	most native speakers don't think they need to learn a second language.
3.	they don't practice changing their speech.
4. Non-native speakers usually use simpler language and more limited vocabulary.	

E DETAILS Choose the correct answers according to the radio show. Then listen again to check your answers. 🎧 2.3

According to the radio host, native English speakers . . .

1. . . . **think / don't think** they need to learn a second language.
2. . . . slow their speech down **more / less** than non-native speakers.
3. . . . **use / don't use** slang or jokes when speaking to non-native English speakers.
4. . . . speak **90 / 19** percent of the time when communicating with non-native speakers.
5. . . . **need / don't need** more time to think before they speak than non-native speakers.

COMMUNICATION TIP

If you agree with someone, tell them. If you **disagree**, say so politely. Use the following language to politely disagree:

I'm afraid I don't agree.

I see what you mean, but I think/don't think that . . .

I understand your point, but I see things a little differently.

F Do you agree or disagree with these statements? Discuss in a group. Use the phrases in the Communication Tip and give reasons for your opinions.

1. People who speak a second language become better communicators in their native language.
2. It is easier to understand non-native English speakers than native English speakers.
3. Native English speakers are very patient with non-native English speakers.

PRONUNCIATION Stress in words with suffixes 🎧 2.5

A suffix is a group of letters added to the end of a word that changes the word's form or meaning. For example, adding *-tion* to the verb *attend* forms the noun *atten<u>tion</u>*. There are patterns of word stress in words with suffixes.

In words ending in *-ion*, *-ian*, and *-ity*, the syllable before the suffix is usually stressed.

re-**vi**-sion   at-**ten**-tion   I-**tal**-ian   **A**-sian   ac-**ti**-vi-ty   u-ni-**ver**-si-ty

G PRONUNCIATION Listen and repeat. Notice the stressed syllable in each word and underline it. Listen again to check your answers. 🎧 2.6

-an or -ian	-ish	-ese
1. In-do-ne-sian	5. Fin-nish	9. Ja-pa-nese
2. Ma-lay-sian	6. Spa-nish	10. Can-to-nese
3. Ko-re-an	7. Tur-kish	11. Vi-et-na-mese
4. Rus-sian	8. En-glish	12. Con-go-lese

H PRONUNCIATION Look at your answers to activity G. Do you see any patterns? Discuss them in a small group and write a rule for each.

1. Languages ending in *-an* or *-ian*: _____

2. Languages ending in *-ish*: _____

3. Languages ending in *-ese*: _____

I PRONUNCIATION Discuss the questions with a partner.

1. What languages do you speak?
2. What languages do you want to speak? Explain.
3. Which languages do you think are the easiest to learn? The hardest? Explain.

J Look at the illustration. Which of the reasons are your top three for learning English? Write them below. Then explain your reasons to a partner.

friends
point of view enjoyment
influence power
acceptance happiness
grow opportunities confidence freedom memories
Why learn a
change language school
understanding jobs
advantages
knowledge

1. _____

2. _____

3. _____

REFLECT Explain the effect of learning a second language.

Answer the questions with a partner or in a small group.

1. Has learning a second language opened your eyes to the world? How?
2. Has learning a second language changed you? Explain.

PREPARE TO WATCH

A VOCABULARY Listen to the words. Then write each word next to its definition. Use a dictionary if necessary. 🎧 2.7

appearance (n)	distinct (adj)	document (v)	expand (v)	inadequate (adj)
contain (v)	diversity (n)	elder (adj)	immense (adj)	values (n)

1. _____ : including many different types of people or things

2. _____ : to record information about something by writing about it

3. _____ : older

4. _____ : extremely large or great

5. _____ : the way that someone or something looks or seems

6. _____ : to include

7. _____ : not good enough, big enough, skilled enough

8. _____ : your beliefs about what is right and wrong, or about what is important in life

9. _____ : to become larger, or to make something larger

10. _____ : not the same, different from others

A family selfie

B **PERSONALIZE** Discuss the questions with a partner.

1. Is there cultural **diversity** in your city?

2. Is your vocabulary adequate or **inadequate** to express what you want to say in English? If it is inadequate, what can you do to **expand** it?

3. What are important **values** in your culture?

C Complete the family tree with the words in your language for each family member. Notice any differences between your language and English.

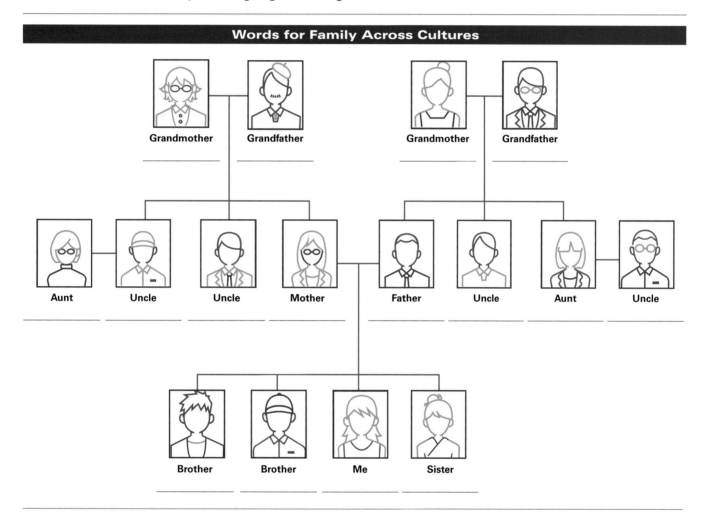

Words for Family Across Cultures

| Grandmother | Grandfather | | Grandmother | Grandfather |

| Aunt | Uncle | Uncle | Mother | Father | Uncle | Aunt | Uncle |

| Brother | Brother | Me | Sister |

REFLECT Discuss how language and culture are related.

You are going to watch a video about language and culture. In a group, compare your family trees and discuss the questions.

1. Are there distinct words in your language for a younger brother/sister or an older brother/ sister? How about other family words? Explain any differences or similarities.

2. Do you think the number of words for family members shows how a culture thinks about family? Explain.

WATCH & SPEAK

EXPLORING LANGUAGE WITH LINGUIST K. DAVID HARRISON

Nick Waikay is interviewed by K. David Harrison in East Sepik Province, Papua New Guinea.

A PREVIEW Watch the excerpt from the video. Each statement has one error. Correct the errors. ▶ 2.1

1. A linguist is a person who speaks many languages.

2. There are more than 17,000 languages in the world.

3. K. David Harrison has learned more than 400 languages.

B PHRASES TO KNOW Work with a partner. Discuss the meaning of these phrases from the video. Then take turns answering the questions.

1. How many of your aunts and uncles are **related to you by blood**? How many **by marriage**?

2. How can learning a language **open doorways to other worlds**?

3. How much time do you spend in the **natural world**?

C MAIN IDEAS Watch the video. Choose two things Harrison says about language. ▶ 2.2

   a. Fewer languages is better for a changing world.

   b. Languages reflect culture and knowledge of the natural world.

   c. Linguists have documented most of the world's languages.

   d. Sayings and proverbs can teach us about culture.

D DETAILS Watch again. Choose the correct answers. ▶ 2.2

   1. English has **one word / several words** for uncle.

   2. The English word *uncle* is inadequate because it refers to **many different people / your mother's elder brother**.

   3. Linguists have not documented **19 / 90** percent of the world's languages.

   4. The Inuit know **more / less** about Arctic ice than climate scientists and meteorologists.

   5. The Inuit have a lot of words to describe sea ice since **they need to survive on the ice / the sea ice is disappearing**.

   6. It is a gift to be bilingual because **it expands your mind / you can travel more easily**.

E DETAILS Watch an excerpt from the video. Match the proverb with the location. Check your answers with a partner. Then discuss the meaning of each one. ▶ 2.3

Proverb	**Location**
1. _____ The early bird catches the worm.	a. Samoa
2. _____ Don't insult the crocodile while you're crossing the river.	b. USA
3. _____ A decision made in the evening is often changed in the morning.	c. Siberia
4. _____ A person's word is an arrow.	d. Ghana

A crocodile on the surface of a river

You are going to participate in a group discussion. Each group member will present a saying or proverb. Use the ideas, vocabulary, and skills from the unit.

F MODEL Listen to students discussing two proverbs. Then write the letter of the proverb next to the situation. Use one of the sayings two times. 🎧 2.8

    a.   Don't insult the crocodile while you're crossing the river.

    b.   A person's word is an arrow.

    1. _____ You need a recommendation letter from a boss that you don't like very much.

    2. _____ Your friend asks you for advice. You don't want to give it to him because it might hurt his feelings.

    3. _____ You have something very important to tell your friend, so you take time preparing exactly what you want to say.

GRAMMAR   Future real conditionals

A **condition** is something that happens and causes something else to happen. The condition is in the *if*-clause, and the result is in the main clause.

> **If you work hard,** *you will succeed.*
>   condition   result

The verb in the *if*-clause is in the simple present. The verb in the main clause is *will* + the base form. It is also possible to use *should* or *might* in the main clause.

> *You **will succeed,** if **you work** hard.*
>   main clause   *if*-clause

> *If you **are not** careful with your words, you **might hurt** someone.*
>   *if*-clause   main clause

G GRAMMAR Complete the sentences with the correct form of the verbs. Then listen and check your answers. 🎧 2.9

    1. I _____ (go) first if nobody _____ (mind).

    2. _____ (not/make) someone angry if you _____ (want) their help.

    3. If someone _____ (be) angry, they _____ (not/help) you.

    4. If you _____ (not/be) careful, your words _____ (miss) their target.

    5. If you _____ (ask) several different people, you _____ probably _____ (get) several different answers.

H GRAMMAR Read the sayings. Complete the sentences to explain what they mean. Then listen and check your answers. 🎧 2.10

1. **Two wrongs don't make a right.**

   If someone _____ (do) something wrong to you, you _____ (not/do) the same back to them.

2. **You catch more flies with honey than with vinegar.**

   If you _____ (need) someone's help, you _____ (be) nice to them.

3. **A decision made in the evening is often changed in the morning.**

   If you _____ (need) to make a decision, you _____ (not/make) it at night. If you _____ (decide) at night, you _____ (probably/regret) your decision in the future.

4. **When in Rome, do as the Romans do.**

   If you _____ (be) in an unfamiliar place, you _____ (be) more successful by following the rules of that place.

An Italian man walking and texting in front of the Colosseum in Rome, Italy

I GRAMMAR Complete the statements with your own ideas. Then share your sentences with a partner.

1. You should listen carefully if _____

2. If you are always late, _____

3. You won't succeed if _____

4. If you exercise every day, _____

SPEAKING SKILL   Take turns in a discussion

It is important to take turns in a discussion or conversation. Each person should have about the same amount of time to speak. You can use the following expressions when taking turns:

Taking the first turn

I'll go first, if you don't mind / if that's OK with everyone.

Offering a turn to someone else

Please go ahead.
No, please. After you.
What do you think? / What are your thoughts?

Changing turns

Anyway, that's what I think / came up with. How about you?
What do you think / did you come up with?
Now it's your turn.

J PLAN Research a saying or proverb in another language. Complete the chart.

Saying/Proverb (English translation)	
Language and Country	
Meaning	

K UNIT TASK Take turns sharing and explaining the meaning of your saying or proverb. As you listen to your classmates, take notes in your notebook about their sayings or proverbs. Which was your favorite?

REFLECT

A Check(✓) the Reflect activities you can do and the academic skills you can use.

☐ give your opinion about learning a language

☐ explain the effect of learning a second language

☐ discuss how language and culture are related

☐ present a saying or proverb

☐ listen for signal words

☐ take turns in a discussion

☐ future real conditionals

☐ support your opinions

B Write the vocabulary words from the unit in the correct column. Add any other words that you learned. Circle words you still need to practice.

NOUN	VERB	ADJECTIVE	ADVERB & OTHER

C Reflect on the ideas in the unit as you answer these questions.

1. Has your view of language and language learning changed? Explain.

_____

_____

_____

2. What ideas or skills in this unit will be most useful to you in the future?

_____

_____

_____

A great white shark follows a marine biologist in a kayak off the coast of South Africa.

CONNECT TO THE TOPIC

1. Do you think this photo is real or fake? Explain.

2. What are examples of fake photos?

PREPARE TO LISTEN

A VOCABULARY Listen to the words. Then match the words with the definitions. Use a dictionary if necessary. 🎧 3.1

1. _____ article (n)   a. to say how good, useful, or successful something is

2. _____ convince (v)   b. the reason for something

3. _____ evaluate (v)   c. to know something because you've seen or heard it before

4. _____ fool (v)   d. a piece of writing in a newspaper, a magazine, or online

5. _____ purpose (n)   e. can be trusted; dependable

6. _____ recognize (v)   f. a person, book, or place that you get information from

7. _____ reliable (adj)   g. to make someone believe that something is true

8. _____ result (n)   h. to trick someone to believe something that is not true

9. _____ source (n)   i. television, radio, newspapers, websites, and magazines

10. _____ the media (n)   j. something that happens because of something else

B Listen to the interview and complete the chart. Then interview a partner and add your and your partner's answers. 🎧 3.2

Have you heard fake news in the last week?

Person	Country	Yes	No
1			
2			
3			
You			
Partner			

CRITICAL THINKING   Evaluate data

When you see a graph with the results of a study, evaluate it carefully to see if it is reliable. Ask:

> *How many people participated in the study? Who were they?*
> *When was the study done?*
> *What is the source of the study?*

C APPLY Look at the graph. Then discuss the questions below with a partner.

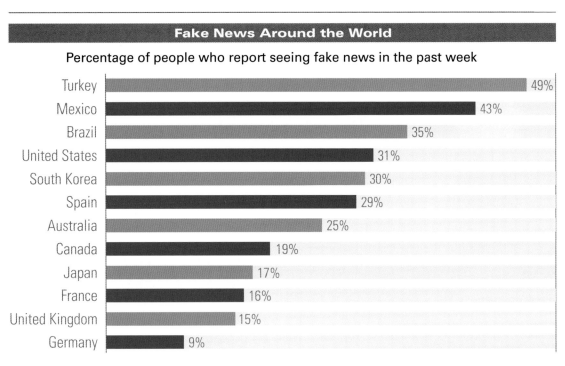

Fake News Around the World

Percentage of people who report seeing fake news in the past week

Country	%
Turkey	49%
Mexico	43%
Brazil	35%
United States	31%
South Korea	30%
Spain	29%
Australia	25%
Canada	19%
Japan	17%
France	16%
United Kingdom	15%
Germany	9%

n = Number of people who responded: 74,000

Source: Reuters Institute Digital News Report 2018

1. How many people were asked about seeing fake news?
2. When was this study done?
3. What is the source of the study?
4. Does the information seem reliable? Explain.

REFLECT   Discuss the issue of fake news.

Before you listen to a discussion about fake news, answer the questions with a partner or in a group.

1. What are some fake news stories you have heard?
2. Do you worry about fake news? Explain.

THE TREE OCTOPUS

A PREVIEW Listen to the beginning of a discussion between a professor and his class. What are they discussing? 🎧 3.3

B PREDICT Choose the percentage of the children you think rated the website "highly reliable." Listen to more of the discussion and check your answer. 🎧 3.4

   a. about 25 percent

   b. about 50 percent

   c. about 75 percent

C MAIN IDEAS Listen to the complete discussion. Choose the main idea. 🎧 3.5

   a. People should not post fake news on the Internet.

   b. Schools need to teach children how to evaluate information from the Internet.

   c. Teachers should not allow their students to read fake news on the Internet.

Hoh Rainforest, Olympic
National Park, Washington, USA

D DETAILS Choose the correct answers. Then listen again to part of the discussion and check your answers. 🎧 3.6

1. The professor read the article _____.
   a. on the Internet
   b. in a textbook
   c. in a newspaper

2. The article said that the octopus lived in _____.
   a. the Pacific Ocean
   b. trees and rivers
   c. the Netherlands

3. According to the article, the octopus is endangered because _____.
   a. the rivers where it lives are drying up
   b. the trees where it lives burned down
   c. people used it for women's hats

4. The story fooled _____.
   a. the professor
   b. the researchers
   c. the children

5. The original idea of the tree octopus came from _____.
   a. the writer of an article
   b. the creator of a website
   c. the children in a study

LISTENING SKILL   Listen for numbers

Numbers are important details, especially in a study. As you listen, take note of numbers and what they refer to. Note if the numbers refer to people, things, or percentages.

7% of 11 and 12 year olds said it was fake
93% said it was reliable

E APPLY Listen to part of the class discussion. Complete the pie charts with the correct numbers. Then check your answers with a partner. 🔊 3.7

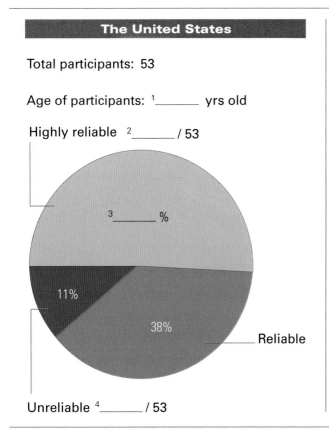

The United States

Total participants: 53

Age of participants: ¹_____ yrs old

Highly reliable ²_____ / 53

³_____ %

11%

38%

Reliable

Unreliable ⁴_____ / 53

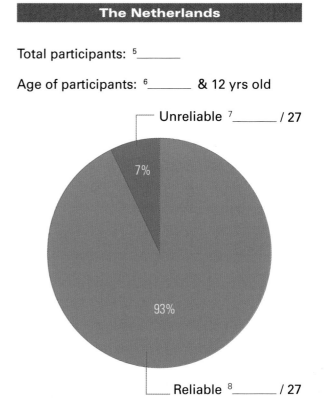

The Netherlands

Total participants: ⁵_____

Age of participants: ⁶_____ & 12 yrs old

Unreliable ⁷_____ / 27

7%

93%

Reliable ⁸_____ / 27

PRONUNCIATION   Rhythm and stress: content vs. structure words 🔊 3.8

Rhythm is the pattern of stressed and unstressed syllables in a sentence. We usually stress content words (nouns, verbs, adjectives, adverbs), *wh-* question words (*what, who*), and negative auxiliaries (*not, can't, didn't*).

We do not usually stress structure words, such as articles (*a, an, the*), prepositions (*in, on*), affirmative auxiliary verbs (*is, did*), or pronouns (*you, he*).

Using correct stress will make your speech easier to understand.

> A: Well it **seems** that it **lives** in the **trees** and **ri**vers of the Pa**ci**fic north**west**.
> B: **What** do **o**ther **sour**ces **say** about the **oc**topus?
> A: **Ac**tually, there **aren't o**ther **sour**ces.

A man takes a selfie with a quokka on Rottnest Island in Australia.

F PRONUNCIATION Underline the words you think will be stressed. Listen and check your answers. Then listen again and mark the stressed syllable in words with more than two syllables. 🎧 3.9

A: Have you ever heard of a quokka?

B: A what?

A: A quokka. Look, it's an endangered animal from Australia. It's really cute. It smiles and poses for selfies with tourists.

B: Let me see that . . . Are you sure this isn't fake news?

A: I don't think so. I saw it on the National Geographic website. That's a reliable source.

B: True. It is really cute, but is it really smiling in the photos?

A: No, I don't think so. I read that it looks like it's smiling when it's hot.

REFLECT   Consider how to deal with fake news.

Answer the questions with a partner. Then share your answers as a class.

1. Does fake news hurt society? Explain.

2. How can schools help students evaluate information from the Internet?

3. Is it possible to stop or decrease the amount of fake news? If so, how?

PREPARE TO WATCH

In 1966, 200 students and teachers in Westall, Australia, saw this unidentified flying object (UFO).

A PREVIEW Look at the photo and read the caption. Discuss the questions with a partner.

1. What is a UFO?

2. Are you or anyone you know interested in UFOs or aliens? Why are people interested in them?

3. Do you believe aliens exist?

B VOCABULARY Listen to the words. Complete the sentences with the correct form of the words. Use a dictionary if necessary. 🔊3.10

aware (adj)	indicate (v)	professional (n)	seem (v)	symbol (n)
common sense (n phr)	journalist (n)	publish (v)	spread (v)	well-known (adj)

1. Li Wei is a _____. She writes for a local newspaper.

2. I'm not _____ of that news site. I've never heard of it before.

3. Most people with _____ would question a story about an octopus that lives in trees.

4. David is excited because a magazine is going to _____ his article.

5. Photos that don't look real often _____ that the news is probably fake.

6. That newspaper is _____, but it is not reliable. Many people read it, but it has a lot of fake news.

7. You shouldn't _____ fake news by sharing it with others.

8. Some photos _____ real, but actually are not.

9. The _____ for "at" is @.

10. She is a respected _____ in the field of marine biology, so I trust her opinion.

C PERSONALIZE Discuss the questions with a partner.

1. Who in your family has **common sense**? Give an example to support your answer.

2. What are some **well-known** and reliable news organizations in your country?

3. Would you like to be a **journalist**?

REFLECT   Interpret an infographic about fake news.

You are going to watch a video about fake news. Look at the infographic. Then answer the questions with a partner.

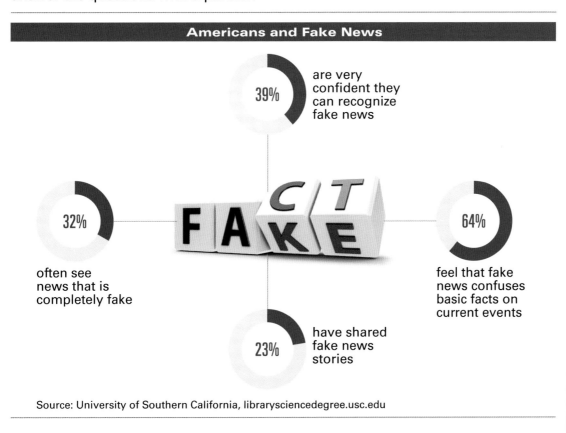

Americans and Fake News

39% are very confident they can recognize fake news

32% often see news that is completely fake

64% feel that fake news confuses basic facts on current events

23% have shared fake news stories

Source: University of Southern California, librarysciencedegree.usc.edu

1. What does the infographic tell us? Is the information reliable?

2. Do any of the percentages surprise you? Which ones?

3. Would the percentages be higher or lower in your home country? Explain.

A SpaceX Falcon 9 rocket lifts off from Vandenberg Air Force Base in California, USA. Some fake news stories about UFOs used photos of this launch.

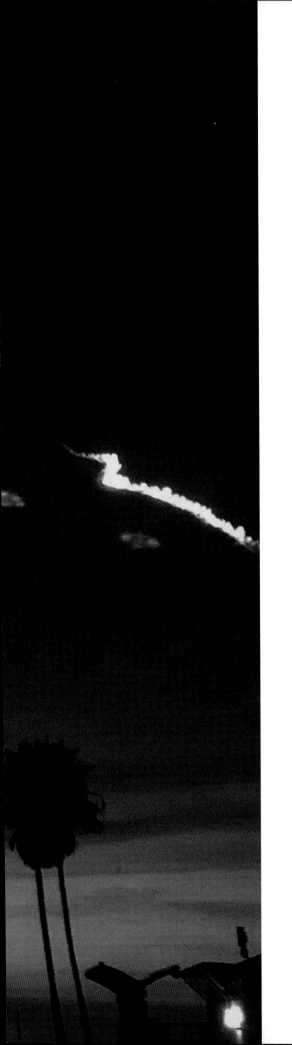

A PREDICT You will watch a video about how to recognize fake news. What four tips do you think you will hear? Discuss and make a list with a partner.

_____

_____

_____

_____

B PHRASES TO KNOW Work with a partner. Discuss the meaning of these phrases from the video. Then take turns answering the questions.

1. How can you **make sure** a website is real?
2. What are some **red flags** that a news story might be fake?
3. Have you ever accidentally **passed** a fake news story **on to** other people?

C Watch the video and take notes. Were your predictions correct? ▶ 3.1

D MAIN IDEAS Choose the main idea.

a. It is hard to recognize if a news story is truth or fiction.

b. There is a lot of fake news in our email inboxes and on social media sites.

c. There are several ways you can recognize fake news in order to avoid spreading it.

LISTENING TIP

When you hear a presentation that includes the steps in a process or a list of information, listen for words such as _the first thing_, _second_, _then_, _next_, and _finally_. These words signal each new step or idea.

E DETAILS Look at your notes. Put the four suggestions in the order of the video.

_____ Check the source.

_____ Check the URL.

_____ Use your common sense.

_____ Check the author.

F Discuss the questions with a partner.

1. Which tips from the video do you already follow?
2. Which tips do you think you will follow in the future?

You are going to find a news story and evaluate its source and the information in the story. Then you will present the story in a small group. Use the ideas, vocabulary, and skills from the unit.

G MODEL Listen to the student's presentation. Write notes in the chart. Discuss your notes with a partner and update your chart. 🎧3.11

Name of article	
Notes about story	
Source (s)	
True or false?	
How do you know?	

Surfers watch dolphins jumping in the waves.

SPEAKING SKILL Ask for and give clarification

Often when listening, you want to be sure you understand. Ask the speaker **clarification questions.**

> *Could you repeat that, please?*
> *Could you say that again, please?*
> *Could you explain what you mean by . . . ?*
> *What do you mean by . . . ?*

Here are phrases to **give clarification**. Use these to be sure others can understand you.

> *Sure. Let me explain.*
> *Sorry, let me put it another way.*

H Listen to the student's presentation again. Check (✓) the expressions in the Speaking Skill box that you hear. 🔊3.11

I **NOTICE THE GRAMMAR** Underline the simple past verbs. Double underline the past continuous verbs. Then tell a partner the difference in meaning.

> Endris was resting on his surfboard when something hit him really hard from below. The shark threw him 15 feet in the air, and he landed on his head. While several of his friends were watching, something even more incredible happened.

GRAMMAR Simple past and past continuous

We use the **simple past** to talk about completed actions that began and ended in the past.

> *Endris **survived** a terrible shark attack.*
>
> *The dolphins **saved** Endris.*

We use the **past continuous** to talk about actions that were in progress at a particular time in the past. We form the past continuous with *was* or *were* and the *-ing* form of the verb.

> *Dolphins **were swimming** around him.*
>
> *Several of his friends **were surfing** nearby.*

You can use *while* and *when* to describe two actions that happened at the same time. One action was in progress (often with *while*) when another action occurred (often with *when*).

> *While Endris **was resting** on his surfboard, something **hit** him really hard from below.*
>
> *Several other surfers **were watching** Endris **when** the shark **attacked**.*

See the Appendices for a list of irregular past verb forms.

J GRAMMAR Complete the sentences with the simple past or past continuous of the verbs in parentheses.

1. Todd Endris _____ (live) through an attack by a 15-foot great white shark.

2. It _____ (be) a beautiful day at the sea.
   The sun _____ (shine), and several dolphins
   _____ (play) in the waves.

3. The dolphins _____ (swim) near Endris when they
   suddenly _____ (form) a circle around the surfer.

4. The dolphins _____ (seem) to protect Todd Endris from the shark.

5. When Todd Endris _____ (get) better, he
   _____ (go) surfing again. He _____
   (not/be) afraid.

K PLAN Choose a news story. Decide whether it is real or fake. Then complete the chart. Practice presenting your story to a partner.

Name of article	
Notes about story	
Sources	
True or false?	
How do you know?	

L UNIT TASK Work in a group. Take turns presenting your stories. In your notebook, create charts like the one in activity K. As you listen to your classmates, take notes in the charts. Which story was the most interesting?

REFLECT

A Check (✓) the Reflect activities you can do and the academic skills you can use.

☐ discuss the issue of fake news
☐ consider how to deal with fake news
☐ interpret an infographic about fake news
☐ evaluate and present a news story

☐ listen for numbers
☐ ask for and give clarification
☐ simple past and past continuous
☐ evaluate data

B Write the vocabulary words from the unit in the correct column. Add any other words that you learned. Circle words you still need to practice.

NOUN	VERB	ADJECTIVE	ADVERB & OTHER

C Reflect on the ideas in the unit as you answer these questions.

1. Will you view news articles differently in the future? If so, how?

_____

_____

_____

2. What ideas or skills in this unit will be most useful to you in the future?

_____

_____

_____

UNIT

4 WHY WE MAKE ART

A man rides a scooter past street art in Aubervilliers, a suburb of Paris, France.

CONNECT TO THE TOPIC

1. Describe the photo. Why do you think this art is here?

2. Where can you see art in your community?

PREPARE TO WATCH

A VOCABULARY Listen to the words. Then read the definitions. Complete the conversation below with the correct form of the words. 🎧 4.1

accessible: (adj) easy to get to, see, or use

expect: (v) to think something will happen

express: (v) to say or communicate something

motivation: (n) the reason someone does something

process: (n) the way of or steps for doing something

public: (adj) shared by all in a place; for anyone to see or use

reflect: (v) to show or be a sign of something

remove: (v) to take something away

society: (n) people in the same community, city, or country

temporary: (adj) happening or lasting for a short time

A: I'm not sure graffiti is really art. What do you think?

B: I think it's art. It's one way people can ¹_____ themselves, and it can be beautiful.

A: I guess. But sometimes graffiti is painted all over city parks or other ²_____ places. The city often ³_____ it soon after it's finished. Real art should last a long time, right?

A narrow alley known for its colorful graffiti in Vila Madalena, a neighborhood in São Paolo, Brazil

B: Hmmm… I don't think it matters. I think art can be
4_____. An ice sculpture doesn't last too long. I think graffiti can say a lot about 5_____. Its images and words often 6_____ the feelings and beliefs of the people who live there.

A: I guess that's true. And it is free! It's 7_____ to everyone. You don't need to pay money or go to a museum to see it.

B PERSONALIZE Answer the questions with a partner.

1. Do you know anyone who **expresses** their ideas through art? If so, what kind of art?
2. Do you like to create art? If so, what is your **motivation** for doing it? If not, why?
3. How **accessible** are art museums in your town? When are they open? How much do they cost?

REFLECT   Evaluate street art.

> You are going to watch a video about a street artist. Answer the questions with a partner.
>
> 1. Do you agree that the graffiti in the photo is art? Explain.
> 2. Describe examples of graffiti or other street art that you have seen. Do you think they are art?

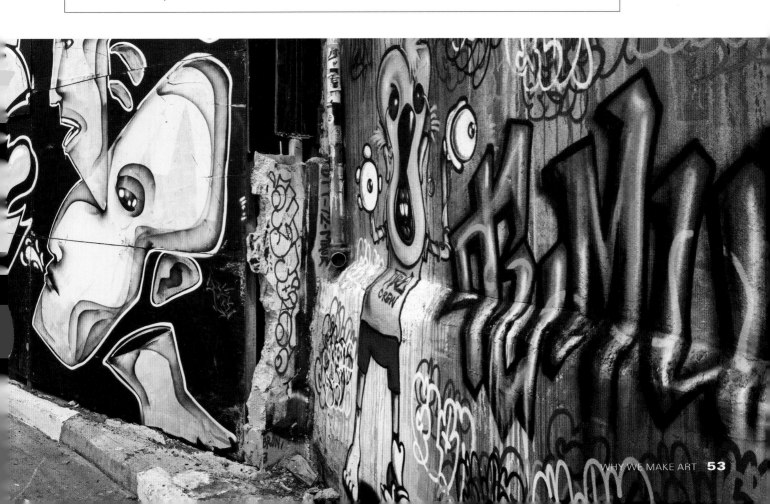

COLORING THE STREETS OF SINGAPORE

A PREDICT What do you think you will learn about Zul? Tell a partner your ideas.

Singaporean street artist Zul (also known as "Zero") with his work

B APPLY With your partner, write *wh-* questions in the chart about what you might learn. Then watch the video and take notes on the answers to your questions. ▶ 4.1

Wh- questions	Answers
1. What is Zul's job?	He is a street artist.
2. Where	
3. How	
4. Why	

C PHRASES TO KNOW Work with a partner. Discuss the meaning of these phrases from the video. Then take turns answering the questions.

1. Do you know anyone who has a **rebellious nature**? What rebellious things do they do?
2. What are examples of **public spaces**? What are specific ones in your town?
3. Do you think artists are **on the fringes** of society? Explain.

D MAIN IDEAS Watch the video again. Choose the three main ideas. ▶ 4.1

a. Street art seems rebellious in Singapore because it is a very neat and organized place.
b. Zul's art is valuable because it disappears as soon as he paints it.
c. Zul wants his art to express what it's like to live in a big city.
d. Zul's art is temporary, and this reflects how quickly things change in Singapore.
e. Making street art in Singapore is dangerous because it's against the law.

E DETAILS Choose the correct answers about Zul.

1. Zul says street art in Singapore is **the same as / better than / different from** street art in other cities.
2. He describes his art as accessible because it's **popular / free / easy to understand**.
3. He thinks removing his art is OK because it is **temporary / ugly / public**.
4. He started doing street art after **high school / college / serving in the military**.
5. Before he started doing street art, Zul was a **student / skateboarder / painter**.
6. He was the first person to get a(n) **show / money / award** from the National Arts Council.
7. He gets the motivation to create more art when the public gives him **attention / money / work**.

Zul at work in his studio

F NOTICE THE GRAMMAR Match the sentence parts. Underline the reason in each completed sentence.

1. Because he grew up in a big city, _____

2. Marco wants to make money, _____

3. This is a good photo _____

a. so he's going to be a graphic artist.

b. because it expresses joy and hope.

c. Zul wants to tell stories about urban life.

GRAMMAR Connecting words for reasons and results

We use *because* to introduce a **reason**. *Because* + subject + verb creates an **adverb clause of reason**. An adverb clause is a dependent clause.

> *Vila Madalena is interesting to visit **because** there is a lot of colorful street art to see.*
>
> reason

Adverb clauses of reason can also begin a sentence.

> ***Because** there is a lot of colorful street art to see, Vila Madalena is interesting to visit.*
>
> reason

We use *so* to introduce a **result**. *So* connects two independent clauses.

> *Street art is illegal in some places, **so** street artists sometimes work at night.*
>
> result

G GRAMMAR Combine the sentences with *because* or *so*. Use the correct punctuation.

1. Street art can be surprising. It's often in places where you don't expect it.

   _____

2. Street art is especially interesting in Singapore. The country is very neat and organized.

   _____

3. There is a law against street art in Singapore. Artists must get permission to paint from the government.

   _____

4. In 2015, Singapore wanted to use art to celebrate its independence. The government asked artists to paint 50 murals.

   _____

5. Street artist Zul grew up in Singapore. His art reflects Singaporean life.

   _____

6. Street artist YC Yip wants to tell stories about Singapore's history. He paints scenes of Chinatown's past.

   _____

7. Little India is an interesting place to visit. There is a lot of street art there.

   _____

8. Singapore changes quickly. People aren't surprised when street art disappears.

   _____

H Answer the questions with a partner. Use *because* or *so* to give reasons and results.

1. Do you like street art?
2. What's your favorite type of art (e.g., sculpture, painting, music)?
3. Do you often visit museums?

CRITICAL THINKING   Analyze motivations

When you *analyze* something, you try to understand it better. A good way to do this is to ask *why* or *how* questions. For example, when you analyze motivations, you can ask questions like *Why did . . . (do) . . . ?* Understanding someone's motivation helps you evaluate their actions.

REFLECT   Analyze the motivations of artists.

Discuss the question with a partner or in a small group.

1. Why do people enjoy art?
2. Why do people create art? Name a few reasons.

PREPARE TO LISTEN

A Look at the photos below of three types of art. Which style do you prefer? Rank them from your most favorite (1) to your least favorite (3). Tell a partner your reasons.

B VOCABULARY Listen to the words. Complete the sentences with the correct form of the words. Use a dictionary if necessary. 4.2

appreciate (v)	direction (n)	entertain (v)	image (n)	influence (v)
definitely (adv)	emotional (adj)	essential (adj)	imagination (n)	passionate (adj)

1. People with depression or other _____ problems often feel better after talking to a therapist.

2. Many people think art education is _____ for young children because it helps them learn.

3. If you want to get a good job as an artist, graphic design is _____ a good career.

4. She was a landscape artist for years. Then she went in a different _____ and became a graphic artist.

5. Video game artists use their _____ to create characters and worlds that we don't see in real life.

6. Learning about a country's art can _____ your ideas about the country.

7. One way to _____ guests from out of town is to take them to a local museum.

8. The City Museum is free, but the city _____ donations from the public.

9. Artists who make art from plastic garbage are often _____ about the environment.

10. Certain _____, such as the lotus flower, are common in Japanese art.

_____   _____   _____

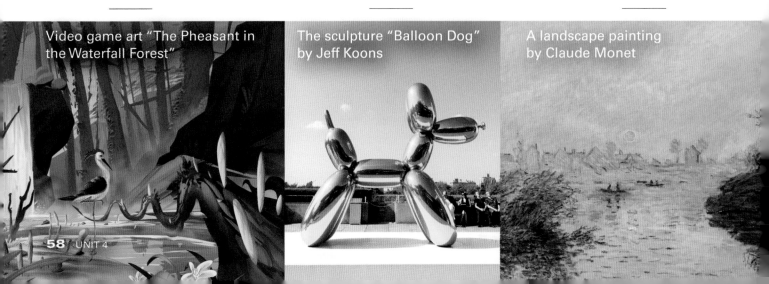

Video game art "The Pheasant in the Waterfall Forest"

The sculpture "Balloon Dog" by Jeff Koons

A landscape painting by Claude Monet

C PERSONALIZE Answer the questions with a partner.

1. What do you **appreciate** about your life?
2. Do you think art classes are **essential** for children?
3. Who **influences** you in your life?

D Look at the chart. Then answer the questions below with a partner.

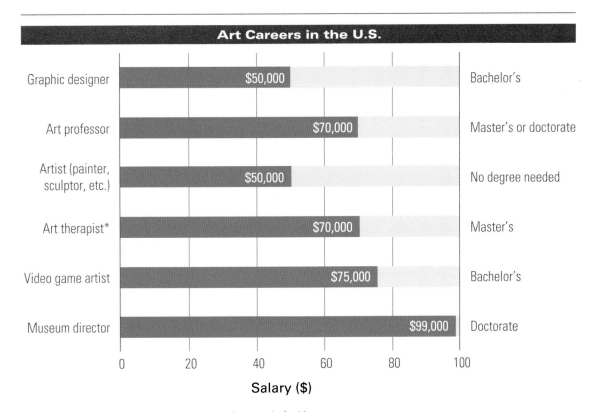

Art Careers in the U.S.

Career	Salary	Education
Graphic designer	$50,000	Bachelor's
Art professor	$70,000	Master's or doctorate
Artist (painter, sculptor, etc.)	$50,000	No degree needed
Art therapist*	$70,000	Master's
Video game artist	$75,000	Bachelor's
Museum director	$99,000	Doctorate

Salary ($)

*therapist (n) a person who uses art to make people feel better

Source: The University Network

1. What does the chart show?
2. Which career pays the most? Which pays least?
3. Which career requires the most education? Which require least education?
4. Why might a video game artist make more money than a museum director?

REFLECT Discuss art careers.

You will listen to four student artists describe their art career choices. Answer the questions in a small group.

1. Which art career in the infographic is the most interesting to you? What influences your choice?
2. How important is salary for your choice of a career? How about the amount of education needed? Explain.

WHY MAKE ART?

A PREVIEW What kind of art is the man creating? Why do you think he makes art?

B PREDICT You will hear a panel discussion with four student artists. Predict the type of art each student will discuss. Brainstorm a list with a partner.

1. _____

2. _____

3. _____

4. _____

C MAIN IDEAS Listen to the panel discussion. Were your predictions correct? Match the speaker with their purpose for doing art. 🎧 4.3

1. _____ David   a. to make people feel better

2. _____ Ana   b. to entertain people

3. _____ Carlos   c. to express imagination

4. _____ Devin   d. to make people aware of the natural world

D DETAILS Listen again and complete the chart. 🎧 4.3

	Kind of artist	Kind of art
David	_____ artist	murals of imaginary _____
Ana	_____ artist	imaginary _____ _____
Carlos	_____ illustrator	pictures of _____
Devin	_____ therapist	painting, sculpture

Alfredo De Los Santos attends an art therapy class in Montrose, New York, after losing a leg while serving in the army.

You are going to choose a work of art to present. You will show it and explain why you chose it. Find information about the art you choose on the Internet. Use the ideas, vocabulary, and skills from the unit.

E MODEL Listen to a student give a presentation about the *Mona Lisa*. Complete the chart. Compare your answers with a partner's. 🎧 4.4

Type of art	
Name of artist	
Opinion of art	
Reason 1	
Reason 2	
Reason 3	

A street artist in Florence, Italy, drawing a picture of the famous painting, the *Mona Lisa*

PRONUNCIATION   Reduced structure words 🔊 4.5

In unstressed structure words, such as articles, prepositions, pronouns, and modals, we often reduce certain sounds. This means that we shorten or omit them.

▸ Often, vowel sounds reduce to schwa /ə/.

> It's <u>a</u> landscape. (a = /ə/)
> My purpose is <u>to</u> educate. (to = /tə/)

▸ Vowels are sometimes omitted.

> You <u>can</u> visit tomorrow. (can = /k'n/)

▸ The consonant sound /h/ at the beginning of pronouns (<u>he</u>, <u>her</u>, <u>him</u>) is often dropped.

> Tell <u>him</u> now. (him = /əm/)
> Give <u>her</u> the answer. (her = /ər/)

F PRONUNCIATION Listen and underline the reduced structure words. Listen again and read along with the speaker. 🔊 4.6

1. Thanks for coming to the first in a series of presentations.
2. What is the main purpose of art, in your opinion?
3. You're shaking your head.
4. For me, the main purpose of art is to entertain people.
5. So to me, art is a kind of therapy.

G PRONUNCIATION Listen to part of the model and write the missing structure words. Then take turns reading Dany's lines aloud with a partner. 🔊 4.7

Dany: Thanks, Mr. Marquez. The work ¹_____ art that I chose is

²_____ painting, The *Mona Lisa*, by Leonardo da Vinci. It's

³_____ really great work of art, ⁴_____ my opinion.

What makes it so great?

Well, one reason is ⁵_____ it's realistic--that is, it looks real. The woman

⁶_____ the picture looks like a real person because ⁷_____

artist used a painting technique called *sfumato*. This means using shades

⁸_____ dark and light paint ⁹_____ certain places, like

around ¹⁰_____ mouth ¹¹_____ eyes. See these places

here? They give shape to ¹²_____ face, so it looks very realistic.

SPEAKING SKILL   Define and explain specific terms

When you talk about a specialized topic, you often need to define and explain special terms. It is important to define these terms in simple language. Here are expressions you can use:

The term . . . refers to/means
This means
. . . is defined as . . .
. . . that is, . . .

. . . the artist used a painting technique called sfumato. ***This means*** *using shades of dark and light paint in certain places, ...*

*Well, one reason is that it's realistic—**that is,** it looks real.*

H PLAN Use the chart to plan your presentation. Include definitions and explanations for any difficult terms.

Type of art	
Name of artist	
Opinion of art	
Reason 1	
Reason 2	
Reason 3	
Difficult terms	

COMMUNICATION TIP

Speakers often check to see if the audience understands them. They ask questions such as:

Are there any questions?
Do you follow me?
Is that clear?

I UNIT TASK Take turns giving your presentations in small groups. As you listen to your classmates, take notes on their presentations. Which work of art did you like the best?

REFLECT

A Check (✓) the Reflect activities you can do and the academic skills you can use.

☐ evaluate street art

☐ analyze the motivations of artists

☐ discuss art careers

☐ give a presentation about a work of art

☐ take notes using a *wh-* question chart

☐ define and explain specific terms

☐ connecting words for reasons and results

☐ analyze motivations

B Write the vocabulary words from the unit in the correct column. Add any other words that you learned. Circle words you still need to practice.

NOUN	VERB	ADJECTIVE	ADVERB & OTHER

C Reflect on the ideas in the unit as you answer these questions.

1. What ideas in the unit were the most interesting to you?

_____

_____

_____

2. What ideas and skills in this unit will be most useful to you in the future?

_____

_____

_____

SKILLS

LISTENING
Listen for time words

SPEAKING
Ask follow-up questions

GRAMMAR
Present perfect

CRITICAL THINKING
Preview a listening

CONNECT TO THE TOPIC

1. Where is the woman? Would you like to visit this place?

2. Do you enjoy exploring new places?

National Geographic Explorer Beverly Joubert runs across red dunes in the Namib Desert in Namibia.

PREPARE TO LISTEN

A VOCABULARY Listen to the words. Complete the questions with the correct form of the words. Use a dictionary if necessary. 🔊 5.1

apparently (adv)	end up (v phr)	expedition (n)	joy (n)	skilled (adj)
assistant (n)	eventually (adv)	illness (n)	region (n)	wealthy (adj)

1. _____, tourists will be able to visit the moon in the next 50 years. Would you go?

2. Have you ever planned to do one thing, but _____ doing something different?

3. Would you like to go on a(n) _____ to the Brazilian rain forest? Explain.

4. Have you ever had a serious _____ and had to stay in a hospital?

5. If you were _____ and could travel anywhere in the world, where would you go?

6. Does traveling bring you _____? If so, how does it make you happy?

7. What does a tour guide need to be _____ at?

8. What do you think a(n) _____ to an explorer does to help the explorer?

9. What tourist attractions does your _____ of the country have?

10. _____, after you stop working, would you like to spend time traveling?

B PERSONALIZE Work with a partner. Take turns asking and answering the questions from activity A.

C Listen to two students discussing explorer Malaika Vaz. Check the things that she has done. 🔊 5.2

Malaika Vaz has...

☐ traveled to the North Pole

☐ gotten a pilot's license

☐ made films

☐ been an actress in a TV series

☐ traveled to the South Pole

☐ ridden a horse from Mongolia to Russia

☐ lived with lions and tigers

National Geographic
Explorer, Malaika Vaz

COMMUNICATION TIP

When we are listening to someone, we use body language and certain sounds and language to **show interest** in what the other person is saying.

Body language	Words and sounds	
Nod your head up and down	*Mmm hmm*	*That's/That sounds interesting.*
Look someone in the eye	*Uh huh*	*That's amazing.*
Raise your eyebrows	*Wow*	*Really? I didn't know that.*

D APPLY Listen to the conversation again. Write the missing words or sounds. 🎧 5.2

A: You know how I love hearing about explorers and adventurers, right?

B: ¹_____

A: Well I saw a program on TV last night about a woman named Malaika Vaz. She's only in her 20s, but she's already done more than most people do in a lifetime.

B: ²_____

A: Yeah, as a teenager, Malaika was the youngest Indian person to travel to both the North Pole and the South Pole . . . and also the youngest to get a pilot's license. And she's traveled on horseback from Mongolia to Russia.

B: ³_____ What has she done recently?

A: She's been making films about wildlife. She is now working on a series about the relationship between humans and lions, leopards, and tigers in India.

B: ⁴_____

A: Yeah, I can't wait to see it.

E Practice the conversation in activity D with a partner. Remember to use body language to show that you are listening.

REFLECT Discuss what it means to be an explorer.

You are going to listen to a conversation about less known explorers from the past. Answer the questions with a partner.

1. What do you think it means to be an explorer?
2. What qualities and skills does an explorer have?

TRAILBLAZERS

Wall art created to celebrate
"International Day of Women and Girls
in Science" in the Canary Islands, Spain.
This mural honors French botanist and
explorer Jeanne Baret (1740-1807).

A Listen to the beginning of a conversation between two students. What are the students going to do? Write your answer. Then share your answer with your class. 🎧 5.3

_____

_____

CRITICAL THINKING   Preview a listening

To preview a listening, think about what you already know about the topic. Look at any photos or available information to get an idea about what you will hear. This will help you understand and make personal connections to the listening.

B PREVIEW Answer the questions. Then discuss your answers with a partner.

1. What does the title "Trailblazers" mean?

_____

2. Look at the photo and read the caption. Why do you think the woman on the wall was a trailblazer?

_____

_____

C MAIN IDEAS Listen to the complete conversation. Choose the two main ideas. 🎧 5.4

a. Jeanne Baret was the first woman to go on an expedition around the world.

b. Jeanne Baret was a housekeeper who worked for a French botanist.

c. Ibn Battuta was a Moroccan who lived during the 14th century.

d. Ibn Battuta was an explorer who traveled all over the world for the joy of it.

e. Jeanne Baret traveled further than Ibn Battuta.

D DETAILS Listen again. Choose the correct answers. 🎧 5.4

1. Jeanne Baret came from a **famous / poor** region of France.

2. Baret was skilled at **using plants as medicine / growing plants**.

3. Baret met Philibert Commerson when she **worked as his housekeeper / saved his life**.

4. Philibert Commerson noticed Baret's knowledge of **local plants / medicine**.

5. Baret's job on the expedition was to **collect plant samples / treat people's illnesses**.

6. Baret had to **be an assistant / pretend to be a man** to go on the expedition.

7. Battuta traveled throughout **Africa, Asia, and southeastern Europe / Morocco and southeast Arabia**.

8. Battuta traveled **12,000 / 120,000** kilometers.

E Listen. Do the voices rise or fall at the end of the sentences? Write ↗ if you hear the voice rise or ↘ if it falls. 🎧 5.5

1. Where was she from?
2. The Soviet Union.
3. Did she spend a long time in space?
4. No, she didn't.

PRONUNCIATION Final intonation 🎧 5.6

Intonation is the rising and falling of the voice. It can change the meaning of a sentence. Final intonation can let you know if a person is making a statement or asking a question.

Here are some common intonation patterns.

Intonation usually falls at the end of **statements** and **wh- questions**.

You go first.

I'm really not ready.

Where was she from?

Intonation usually rises at the end of **yes/no questions**.

Does everyone know what to do?

You can make a sentence into a *yes/no* question with rising intonation at the end of the sentence.

She traveled around the world?

Valentina Tereshkova, a Soviet cosmonaut and the first woman to visit outer space (1963)

F PRONUNCIATION Draw an ↗ or ↘ at the end of each sentence to predict the final intonation. Then listen to the conversation about Valentina Tereshkova and check your answers. 🎧 5.7

A: Did you choose someone for your report? ↗

B: Yes. ↘

A: Who did you choose?

B: Valentina Tereshkova.

A: What did she do?

B: She was the first woman to travel into outer space.

A: Really? That's interesting. Where was she from?

B: The Soviet Union.

A: When did she go?

B: In 1963.

A: Did she spend a long time in space?

B: No. She spent just 70 hours in space. She circled Earth 48 times.

A: Did she ever go into space again?

B: No, she didn't. She became a politician.

G Write three questions to ask Valentina Tereshkova, Jeanne Baret, and/or Ibn Battuta. Practice asking and answering the questions with a partner. If you don't know an answer, create one or find it on the Internet.

> *A: Where did Jeanne Baret end up living after her expedition?* ↘
>
> *B: In Paris.* ↘

REFLECT   Consider explorers, past and present.

1. How are the four explorers you've just learned about unusual?
2. How are the three explorers from the past (Jeanne Baret, Ibn Battuta, and Valentina Tereshkova) different from Malaika Vaz, or other modern explorers? How are they similar?

PREPARE TO WATCH

A VOCABULARY Listen to the words. Then complete the sentences with the correct form of the words. Use a dictionary if necessary. 🔊 5.8

alert (v)	disaster (n)	landscape (n)	mission (n)	survive (v)
crew (n)	failure (n)	leadership (n)	rescue (v)	trap (v)

1. When a storm is coming, the weather service _____ the public.

2. The expedition was a _____ because they were not able to achieve their goals.

3. Pierre sailed around the world with a _____ of only two other people.

4. The _____ in Scotland is beautiful. I took hundreds of photos of hills with sheep when I was there.

5. Under his _____, we will be successful. He is a great problem solver and knows how to get people to follow him.

6. Wildlife workers _____ the snake in a bag and moved it to a safe place.

7. The team's _____ was to rescue the children in the cave.

8. The skater fell through the ice on the lake, but fortunately the police were able to _____ him.

9. They were very lucky to _____ the crash.

10. Every year, people deal with terrible natural _____, such as earthquakes and hurricanes.

B PERSONALIZE Discuss these questions with a partner.

1. Have you ever experienced a **failure**? What happened and what did you learn?

2. When you travel, do you usually take photos of people, **landscapes**, or both? Which do you think is more interesting to photograph?

3. What are important **leadership** skills? Do you think you have these skills?

4. What sort of natural **disasters** does your city or country deal with? What are some examples?

Travelers watch from a ship as it goes through pack ice in Antarctica.

C Listen to a short lecture about Antarctica. Read the statements. Write T for *True* or F for *False*. ▶ 5.9

1. _____ Some explorers died exploring Antarctica in the early 20th century.

2. _____ At 2,300 meters high, on average, Antarctica is the highest continent.

3. _____ Antarctica contains 98 percent of Earth's fresh water.

4. _____ Antarctica has a lot of rain and snowfall.

5. _____ Because of the height and dryness, it is hard to breathe on Antarctica.

6. _____ It is difficult to eat enough to remain healthy while crossing Antarctica.

REFLECT   Discuss exploration, past and present.

You are going to watch a video about a historical expedition to Antarctica. Discuss the questions with a partner.

1. What do you think an expedition to Antarctica was like in the past? What do you think an expedition to Antarctica is like today?

2. What qualities and skills do you think a leader of an expedition to Antarctica needed in the past? What qualities and skills would a leader need today?

A TALE OF TWO EXPLORERS

Tourists explore the beach on Elephant Island, Antarctica, where Shackleton left for South Georgia.

A PREDICT Look at the title, photo, captions, and map. Do you think Shackleton's expedition was a success or a failure? Discuss your answer with a partner. Then watch the video and check your prediction. ▶ 5.1

B MAIN IDEAS Choose the main idea of the video.

   a. Shackleton was an unsuccessful leader because he was unable to complete his expedition, and he put the lives of his crew at risk.

   b. Shackleton was a successful leader because he led his crew under very difficult conditions and managed to rescue all of them.

LISTENING SKILL   Listen for time words

When listening to a narrative (story) about a past event, pay attention to time words and time expressions. These will help you understand the order of events.

Common time words: *after, before, since, until, when, while*

Prepositional phrases: *in* (+ year/month), *on* (+ day)

Adverbs: *eventually, finally*

C DETAILS Watch the excerpt from the video. Complete the map with the correct dates and numbers. ▶ 5.2

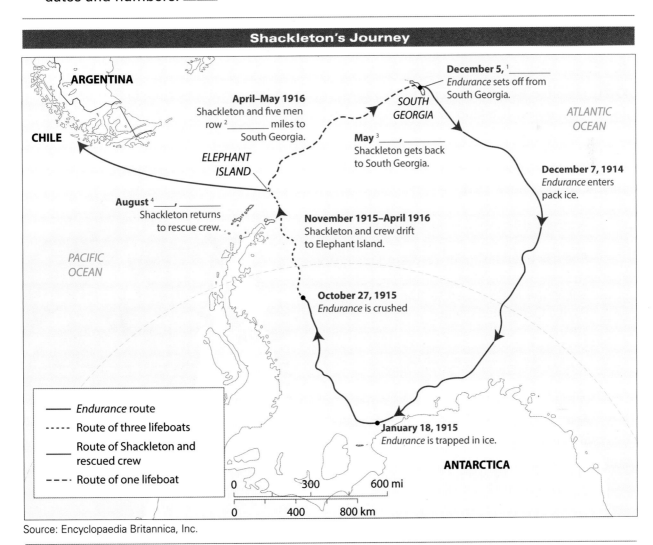

Shackleton's Journey

ARGENTINA

CHILE

April–May 1916
Shackleton and five men row ² _____ miles to South Georgia.

ELEPHANT ISLAND

August ⁴____, _____
Shackleton returns to rescue crew.

PACIFIC OCEAN

SOUTH GEORGIA

May ³____, _____
Shackleton gets back to South Georgia.

December 5, ¹ _____
Endurance sets off from South Georgia.

ATLANTIC OCEAN

December 7, 1914
Endurance enters pack ice.

November 1915–April 1916
Shackleton and crew drift to Elephant Island.

October 27, 1915
Endurance is crushed

January 18, 1915
Endurance is trapped in ice.

ANTARCTICA

——— *Endurance* route
----- Route of three lifeboats
____ Route of Shackleton and rescued crew
---- Route of one lifeboat

0   300   600 mi
0   400   800 km

Source: Encyclopaedia Britannica, Inc.

D APPLY Read the excerpts from the video and complete with the missing time words. Then watch and check your answers. ▶ 5.3

1. He completed the first documented crossing of South Georgia ¹_____ 1916,
   ²_____ on a mission to rescue stranded members of his ill-fated Trans-Antarctic Expedition aboard the *Endurance*. ³_____ they set off from South Georgia ⁴_____ 1914, the *Endurance* crew was taking a huge risk, one unimaginable today.

2. They ⁵_____ found refuge on a tiny island, off the tip of the Antarctic peninsula. They were ⁶_____ on dry ground. Today, we might use modern tech to call for help, but Shackleton didn't have that option. So, he packed a few of his men in a lifeboat to look for rescue. ⁷_____ an 800-mile journey, Shackleton returned to South Georgia. It had been 17 months ⁸_____ the *Endurance* first set sail.

UNIT TASK   Role-play an interview with an explorer.

You are going to pretend to be a famous explorer. You will research the explorer and role-play an interview. Use the ideas, vocabulary, and skills from the unit.

E MODEL Listen to two students perform a role-play of an interview with Amelia Earhart. Imagine this interview is taking place in 1936. Write T for *True*, F for *False*, or NG for *Not Given*. 🎧 5.10

Roleplay of an interview, 1936

1. _____ Amelia Earhart is an American pilot.

2. _____ She has been flying for 23 years.

3. _____ She is the first woman to cross the Pacific Ocean in a plane.

4. _____ She has flown alone across North America and the Atlantic and Pacific Oceans.

5. _____ While she was flying alone across the Atlantic Ocean, she landed her plane in England.

6. _____ She plans to fly along the equator around the world.

Amelia Earhart

GRAMMAR   Present perfect

We form the present perfect with *have* or *has* plus the past participle of the main verb.
We use the present perfect for the following:

▸ Events that take place sometime in the past, but the exact time is not mentioned. If the time is
mentioned, we use the simple past.

   A: **Have** you ever **gone** skydiving.

   B: No, I **haven't**. I**'ve** never **done** that. OR Yes, I **have**. I went last year.

▸ An event that began in the past and continues up to the present. We often use *for* + a period of
time and *since* + a past time to show length of time.

   A: How long **have** you **been** a pilot?

   B: I**'ve been** a pilot **for two years**. OR I**'ve been** a pilot **since I was 20 years old**.

F   GRAMMAR Read the excerpts from the model. Complete the sentences with the correct
form of the present perfect. Then listen and check your answers. 🔊 5.11

1.   **Interviewer:** How long ¹_____ (you/be) a pilot?

     Earhart: Since I was 23 years old. I ²_____ (be) a pilot for about 17 years.

2.   **Interviewer:** ³_____ (you/ever/be) scared?

     Earhart Oh, yes, many times. Things ⁴_____ (go) wrong on several of my

     flights, but fortunately, I ⁵_____ (manage) to survive.

3.   **Interviewer:** So what's next for you? ⁶_____ (you/decide) on your next

     challenge?

     Earhart: Yes, I ⁷_____. I'm planning a flight around the world. I'm going to fly along the

     equator.

     Interviewer: ⁸_____ (anyone/ever/do) that before?

     Earhart: No. I will be the first, and not the first woman, but the first person, male or female.

G   GRAMMAR Complete the conversations. Write about yourself. Use the present perfect.
Then ask a partner the questions.

1.   **A:** How long _____ (you/be) a student?

     B: I _____ (be) a student for _____ years, since _____.

2.   **A:** What interesting place _____ (you/visit)?

     B: The most interesting place that I _____ (visit) is _____.

3.   **A:** Where _____ (you/never/travel)?

     B: I _____ (never/travel) to _____, but I hope to

     go one day!

SPEAKING SKILL Ask follow-up questions

One way to show that you are a good listener is to ask follow-up questions. Follow-up questions are based on the information the other person gives. Ask these questions to encourage the other person to continue talking.

A: *My name is Amelia Earhart, and I'm an American pilot.*
B: **How long have you been a pilot?**
A: *Since I was 23 years old. I've been a pilot for about 17 years.*
B: **How did you learn to fly?**

H APPLY Take turns asking and answering the questions with a partner. Ask follow-up questions.

1. Have you ever dreamed of living somewhere else? Where?

2. What places have you visited in your country?

3. What interesting natural or historical places have you seen?

4. What is an activity that you've never done but would like to do?

I PLAN Research an explorer for your role-play. If you choose an explorer who is dead, you will pretend that you are in the past. Take notes in the chart on the explorer's life.

Name and country	
Places explored	
Achievements	

J PLAN Exchange notes from activity I with a partner. Based on the information in the chart, write questions to ask during the interview.

1. _____

2. _____

3. _____

K UNIT TASK Take turns performing your role-play with your partner. Ask follow-up questions.

A: *What is your name and where are you from?*
B: *My name is Ibn Battuta. I'm from Morocco.*
A: *Oh, that's interesting. What city in Morocco are you from?*

REFLECT

A Check (✓) the Reflect activities you can do and the academic skills you can use.

☐ discuss what it means to be an explorer   ☐ listen for time words

☐ consider explorers, past and present   ☐ ask follow-up questions

☐ discuss exploration, past and present   ☐ present perfect

☐ role-play an interview with an explorer   ☐ preview a listening

B Write the vocabulary words from the unit in the correct column. Add any other words that you learned. Circle words you still need to practice.

NOUN	VERB	ADJECTIVE	ADVERB & OTHER

C Reflect on the ideas in the unit as you answer these questions.

1. Which explorer from the unit was the most interesting to you? Explain.

_____

_____

_____

2. What ideas or skills in this unit will be most useful to you in the future?

_____

_____

_____

6 | THE VALUE OF MEMORY

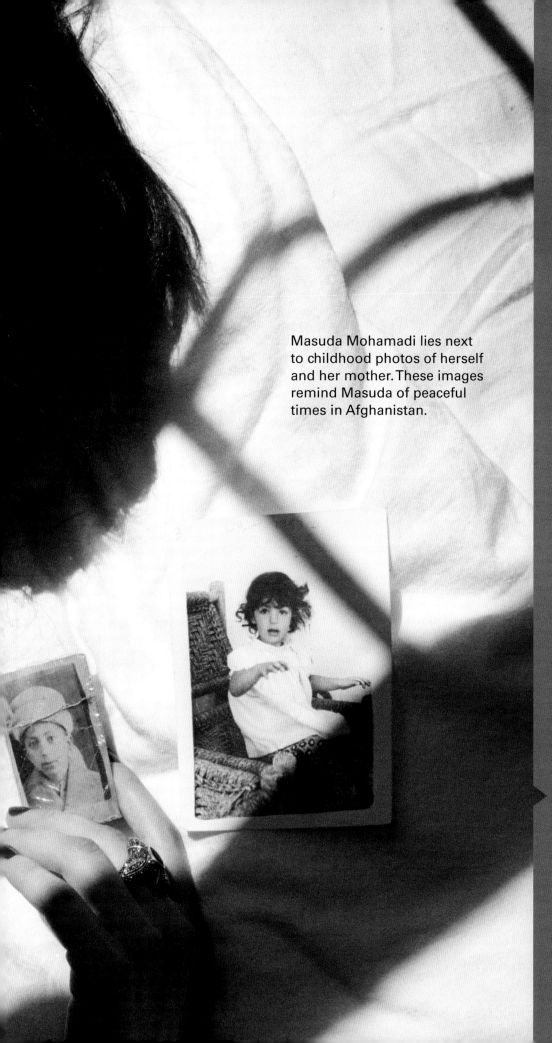

Masuda Mohamadi lies next to childhood photos of herself and her mother. These images remind Masuda of peaceful times in Afghanistan.

CONNECT TO THE TOPIC

1. Describe the photo. What do you think the photo is trying to express?

2. How often do you look at photos of friends and family? How does it make you feel?

PREPARE TO LISTEN

A VOCABULARY Listen to the words. Match the words with the definitions. Use a dictionary if necessary. 6.1

1. ____ absolutely (adv)   a. to keep something safe

2. ____ ahead (prep)   b. the way someone does and says things

3. ____ behavior (n)   c. noticing that something is happening

4. ____ conscious (adj)   d. the way things are at a specific time and place

5. ____ painful (adj)   e. the study of the mind

6. ____ personality (n)   f. a friendship between two people

7. ____ protect (v)   g. in the future; in front

8. ____ psychology (n)   h. certainly

9. ____ relationship (n)   i. what a person is like

10. ____ situation (n)   j. causing someone to feel hurt or sad

B Complete the information with the correct form of the words. Then listen and check your answers. 6.2

absolutely	painful	protect	psychology	relationships

Hyperthymesia

Can you remember what you had for breakfast this morning? A week ago? Ten years ago? Probably not. However, some people can remember ¹_____ every personal event and experience they've had since childhood. They have a rare condition called *hyperthymesia*.

How does hyperthymesia work? We don't know, but many professors of ²_____ are trying to find out. They want to know how the brains of people with hyperthymesia are different from others.

You might think that remembering every detail of your life would be great, but people with this condition also can't forget negative or ³_____ memories. Never forgetting fights, for example, could affect your ⁴ _____ with family and friends. There may be a reason we forget these details. Some say that forgetting such memories may actually ⁵ _____ us from difficulties and help us to be happier.

C PERSONALIZE Discuss these questions with a partner.

1. Did your parents ever punish you for bad **behavior**?
2. How would your friends and family describe your **personality**?
3. What types of **situations** have you been in that you would like to forget?

COMMUNICATION TIP

When someone talks about a negative or painful event, you can use certain phrases to show that you are paying attention and understand the speaker's feelings.

Oh no!

That's terrible/awful!

I'm so sorry.

D Complete the conversation with phrases from the Communication Tip. Then practice with a partner.

A: Do you want to go for a bike ride with me this weekend?

B: Oh, no thanks. I don't really like riding bikes.

A: Really? Why not?

B: I had a negative experience riding a bike when I was young.

A: ¹_____ What happened?

B: Well, I was riding by a big group of kids from my school. They weren't very nice kids. They were mean to the other kids, and they liked to laugh at them. While I was riding by, I hit a rock and fell off my bike.

A: ²_____ What did the kids do?

B: They laughed at me and made fun of me for the rest of the school year.

A: ³_____ Do you want to go for a walk instead?

B: Sure, that sounds great.

REFLECT Discuss how our memories affect our behavior.

You are going to listen to a lecture about how your memories relate to your behavior. Answer these questions.

1. How did the speaker's memory of a childhood experience affect her behavior?
2. Do any of your memories affect your behavior now?

School girls in Japan riding bikes

YOUR MEMORIES AND YOU

A skateboarder falling off of his skateboard

A PREVIEW Describe the photo to a partner. Do you think this experience affected the skateboarder's future behavior?

B PHRASES TO KNOW Work with a partner. Discuss the meaning of these phrases from the lecture. Then take turns answering the questions.

1. Do you **live in the moment**?

2. Do you have memories of **the distant past**? What is an example of one?

3. How might painful memories be good for us or **serve a purpose**?

C MAIN IDEAS Listen to the lecture and choose the three main ideas. 🎧 6.3

    a. We remember negative memories better than positive memories.

    b. Our memories serve a purpose.

    c. Our memories of events change over time.

    d. Scientists are researching ways to improve memory.

    e. Our memories make us who we are.

D DETAILS Listen again. Complete the sentences with words from the lecture. 🎧 6.3

    1. Memory includes things you've done and things you've _____.

    2. Bad memories may stop us from going into dangerous _____ or forming unhealthy _____ with people.

    3. _____ people remember negative events better than _____ people do.

    4. Older people generally live in the _____ and focus on positive memories.

    5. Your past experiences are part of you even if you don't have _____ memories of them.

LISTENING SKILL Distinguish facts from opinions

It is important to recognize the difference between facts and opinions. **Facts** are things that are true or that you can prove. They sometimes include numbers, names, and dates. **Opinions** are beliefs about things.

    Fact: *Memories are part of who we are.*
    Opinion: *I think people should try to forget bad memories.*

These phrases often introduce opinions:
    I believe/think . . .   *In my opinion, . . .*
    This may/might/could mean . . .   *This probably/possibly means . . .*
    This suggests . . .   *One theory is . . .*

E APPLY Read the statements. Are they facts or opinions? Write F for *Fact* or O for *Opinion*.

    1. _____ I think my experiences make me who I am.

    2. _____ Memory includes all the things you've done and learned.

    3. _____ Many studies find that we remember negative events better than positive ones.

    4. _____ Painful memories often cause psychological and even physical problems.

    5. _____ Carstensen's theory is that younger people need to remember negative situations to protect themselves.

    6. _____ Our memories affect our personalities, our behavior, and the decisions we make.

PRONUNCIATION   Focus words 🎧6.4

A **focus word** is the most important word in a phrase or sentence. It is stressed more than any other word in the phrase or sentence. The focus word often gives new information and is usually the last content word in a phrase or sentence.

*Our professor talked about the importance of **me**mories.*

In some cases, the focus word is the word that corrects or contrasts with previous information.

*A: The professor said that feelings aren't im**por**tant.*
*B: Actually, he said that feelings **are** important.*

F PRONUNCIATION Listen to the sentences and notice the stress on the underlined focus words. Then practice saying them with a partner. 🎧6.5

1. What creates your perso**na**lity?

2. Negative memories may serve a **pur**pose.

3. They may help us avoid repeating mi**stakes**.

4. They keep us away from dangerous situ**a**tions.

5. Negative memories might help young people prepare for future **dan**gers.

6. Our memories are **part** of us. They make us who we **are**.

7. A: Do you remember that time I fell **skate**boarding?

   B: **No**, but I remember when **I** fell.

8. A: Is the psychology class to**night**?

   B: **No**. It's to**mor**row night.

G PRONUNCIATION Listen and underline the focus words in each phrase or sentence. The first three lines have been done. 🎧6.6

A: According to the <u>professor</u>, memories are not just the things that <u>happened</u>.

   They are also the <u>feelings</u> involved with the things that happened.

B: <u>Right</u>. For <u>example</u>, a memory includes whether you had <u>fun</u>.

A: It also includes how an event affected a relationship.

B: And he said we may remember positive events better.

A: Actually, he said we may remember negative events better.

B: Really?

A: Yes. Remembering negative events can help us survive.

B: Oh yeah, and older people remember them more.

A: No, younger people remember them more.

H Do you agree or disagree with these ideas from the lecture? Write A for *Agree* or D for *Disagree*. Then share your opinions with a partner.

1. _____ The things that you've learned help make you who you are.

2. _____ We may remember negative events better than positive ones because we pay attention to them.

3. _____ Negative memories may help us survive.

CRITICAL THINKING   Categorize ideas

When you categorize ideas, you organize them by type. For example, you might categorize positive and negative ideas or ideas you like and ideas you don't like. Categorizing helps you organize ideas so you can study or analyze them more easily.

I Brainstorm positive and negative memories you have. Write them in the chart.

Positive memories	Negative memories

REFLECT   Relate ideas about memory to your life.

Think about a memory from activity I. Answer the questions. Then discuss them with a partner.

1. What was the event? What do you remember about it?

_____

2. What feelings do you connect to it?

_____

3. Has it influenced your personality?

_____

PREPARE TO WATCH

A VOCABULARY Listen to the words. Write the correct word next to each definition. Use a dictionary if necessary. 🎧 6.7

| awful (adj) | experience (n) | individual (adj) | pleasure (n) | symptom (n) |
| depression (n) | experiment (n) | mood (n) | recover (v) | technique (n) |

1. _____ relating to only one person, place, or thing

2. _____ a sign of an illness or disease

3. _____ a scientific test to find out what happens in a situation

4. _____ a way of doing something

5. _____ a feeling of great sadness

6. _____ something that happens to you

7. _____ a feeling of happiness

8. _____ the way someone feels

9. _____ to become well again

10. _____ very bad

B Complete the paragraph with the correct form of the words from activity A.

Depression

^1_____ is an illness that affects a person's ^2_____. The main
^3_____ of this illness is a feeling of great sadness. In addition, people who have this
illness may not be able to look for things that might make them feel good. They can't feel
^4_____. People without this illness usually look for foods, activities, and experiences that
they enjoy. They also feel hopeful about the future. Doctors use different ^5_____ to try
to help people ^6_____ from this illness. Sometimes they give patients medication. They
might also ask their patients to get more exercise, eat well, and talk to a therapist. One brain scientist
is doing ^7_____ to try to find a way to use memories to help people with depression.

C PERSONALIZE Discuss the questions with a partner.

1. What kinds of **experiences** have positive effects on your **mood**? Negative effects?

2. What **techniques** do you use to remember facts for a test?

3. How long does it usually take you to **recover** from a cold?

A man falling off
of his surfboard

D Look at the infographic. Which techniques do you think are best for forgetting a bad memory? Rank them from 1 to 5 (1 = the best). Then discuss your ideas with a partner.

How to Forget a Bad Memory

_____ Write about the memory. | _____ Push the bad memory away. | _____ Connect something positive to the bad memory. | _____ Forget the details connected to the bad memory. | _____ Keep yourself busy.

REFLECT Consider reasons for removing a memory.

You are going to watch a video about recent research into memories. If it were possible, would you ask a doctor to remove a memory? Complete the chart with reasons why it might be a good idea or a bad idea.

Good idea to remove a memory	Bad idea to remove a memory

WHAT IF WE COULD
TURN OUR MEMORIES ON OR OFF?

A PREDICT Why do you think a scientist might be interested in trying to turn memories on and off? Share your ideas with your class.

National Geographic Explorer Steve Ramirez at Massachusetts Institute of Technology (MIT), where he is doing research on the brain and memories

B MAIN IDEAS Watch the video. Choose the three main ideas. ▶ 6.1

 a. We might be able to help certain people by turning their memories on and off.

 b. Ramirez has helped some people with Alzheimer's disease.

 c. Ramirez and his team tested their technique on mice.

 d. The experiment showed that memories do not affect our mood.

 e. Turning on a good memory helped mice that had a symptom of depression.

C DETAILS Watch the video again. Write T for *True* or F for *False*. ▶ 6.1

 1. _____ Ramirez and his team have found a way to locate the specific brain cells that contain memories.

 2. _____ Ramirez and his team can turn those memories on and off in mice.

 3. _____ Ramirez and his team let mice choose between sugar water and milk.

 4. _____ Mice that had a symptom of depression chose sugar water most of the time.

 5. _____ When Ramirez and his team turned on a positive memory for the mice with depression, they chose sugar water 80 percent of the time.

 6. _____ When Ramirez and his team turned on a good memory over and over again, depression symptoms increased.

D Read the statements. Are they facts or opinions? Write F for *Fact* or O for *Opinion*.

 1. _____ Memories are stored in a part of the brain called the hippocampus.

 2. _____ The team thought that turning on positive memories could help the mice.

 3. _____ Animals that don't show symptoms associated with depression choose sugar water about 80 percent of the time.

 4. _____ Ramirez's work could improve many people's lives.

 5. _____ Activating a positive memory again and again increased the number of new brain cells.

E What are some memories you would turn on again and again? Write your ideas. Then share them with a partner.

_____

_____

_____

You are going to debate this question: "Should we allow doctors to change people's memories (remove bad memories, add good memories, turn memories on and off)?" Use the ideas, vocabulary, and skills from the unit.

F MODEL Listen to students debate the question: "Should scientists make a pill that helps people remember everything?" Complete the chart. 🎧 6.8

	Jason	Nina
For or against?		
Reason 1		
Reason 2		
Reason 3		

SPEAKING SKILL   Present arguments for and against

When you argue for or against something, you need to show its advantages and disadvantages. You can use phrases like these:

The main advantage/disadvantage is that . . .
Another advantage/disadvantage is that . . .

G APPLY Use phrases from the Speaking Skill box to complete these statements about a memory pill.

1. _____ it would make test taking easier.

2. _____ we could help people with Alzheimer's disease.

3. _____ we don't know how a memory pill will affect people's brains.

4. _____ it's good to forget certain things.

In a debate, speakers should be polite as they give different opinions.

To **agree**, you can say:

I agree that . . ./It's true that . . .

To **disagree**, you can say:

That's an interesting point, but I disagree./I'm not sure I agree.

GRAMMAR Unreal present and future conditional

We use unreal present and future conditional to talk about untrue, imagined, or impossible situations and their results in the present or future.

Use the simple past in the *if*-clause (or condition clause) and *would/could/might (not)* + verb in the result clause. *Could* or *might* show possibility.

> If we **removed** all our memories, our personalities **might change**.
>   *if*-clause   result clause

> If we **turned on** positive memories in people with depression, we **could help** them.
>   *if*-clause   result clause

The *if*-clause can also come second in a sentence.

> Our personalities might change **if we removed all our memories**.

H GRAMMAR Complete the sentences with the correct forms of the verbs in parentheses. There may be more than one answer.

1. If a memory-erasing pill _____ (exist), I _____ (not take) it.

2. If doctors _____ (turn) on the memories of people with Alzheimer's disease, those people _____ (get) their lives back.

3. You _____ (not be) able to protect yourself from danger if you _____ (delete) all your bad memories.

4. If scientists _____ (be) able to change people's memories, criminals _____ (try) to give people fake memories.

5. You _____ (lose) a good memory if a doctor _____ (make) a mistake.

6. People with PTSD _____ (have) happier lives if doctors _____ (remove) their worst memories.

I GRAMMAR Complete the sentences with your own ideas. Then share with a partner.

1. If we only remembered good things, _____.

2. If we only remembered bad things, _____.

3. I would remove a memory if _____.

4. I would ask my teacher for help if _____.

5. If I could do anything right now, _____.

J Complete the chart with ideas from the unit and your own ideas.

Reasons for changing people's memories	Reasons against changing people's memories

K PLAN Choose a side based on your chart in activity J. Write the three strongest reasons in the chart. Then add details to support the reasons.

Strongest reasons	Details

L UNIT TASK Find a partner with a different opinion. Debate your partner. Use the phrases in the Communication Tip to agree or disagree. As you listen to your partner, take notes in the chart. Who won your debate?

Reasons	Details

REFLECT

A Check (✓) the Reflect activities you can do and the academic skills you can use.

☐ discuss how our memories affect our behavior   ☐ distinguish facts from opinions

☐ relate ideas about memory to your life   ☐ present arguments for and against

☐ consider reasons for removing a memory   ☐ unreal present and future conditional

☐ debate ideas about changing memories   ☐ categorize ideas

B Write the vocabulary words from the unit in the correct column. Add any other words that you learned. Circle words you still need to practice.

NOUN	VERB	ADJECTIVE	ADVERB & OTHER

C Reflect on the ideas in the unit as you answer these questions.

1. Have your knowledge and thoughts about memory changed? Explain.

   _____

   _____

   _____

2. What ideas or skills in this unit will be most useful to you in the future?

   _____

   _____

   _____

UNIT 7 | GET CREATIVE

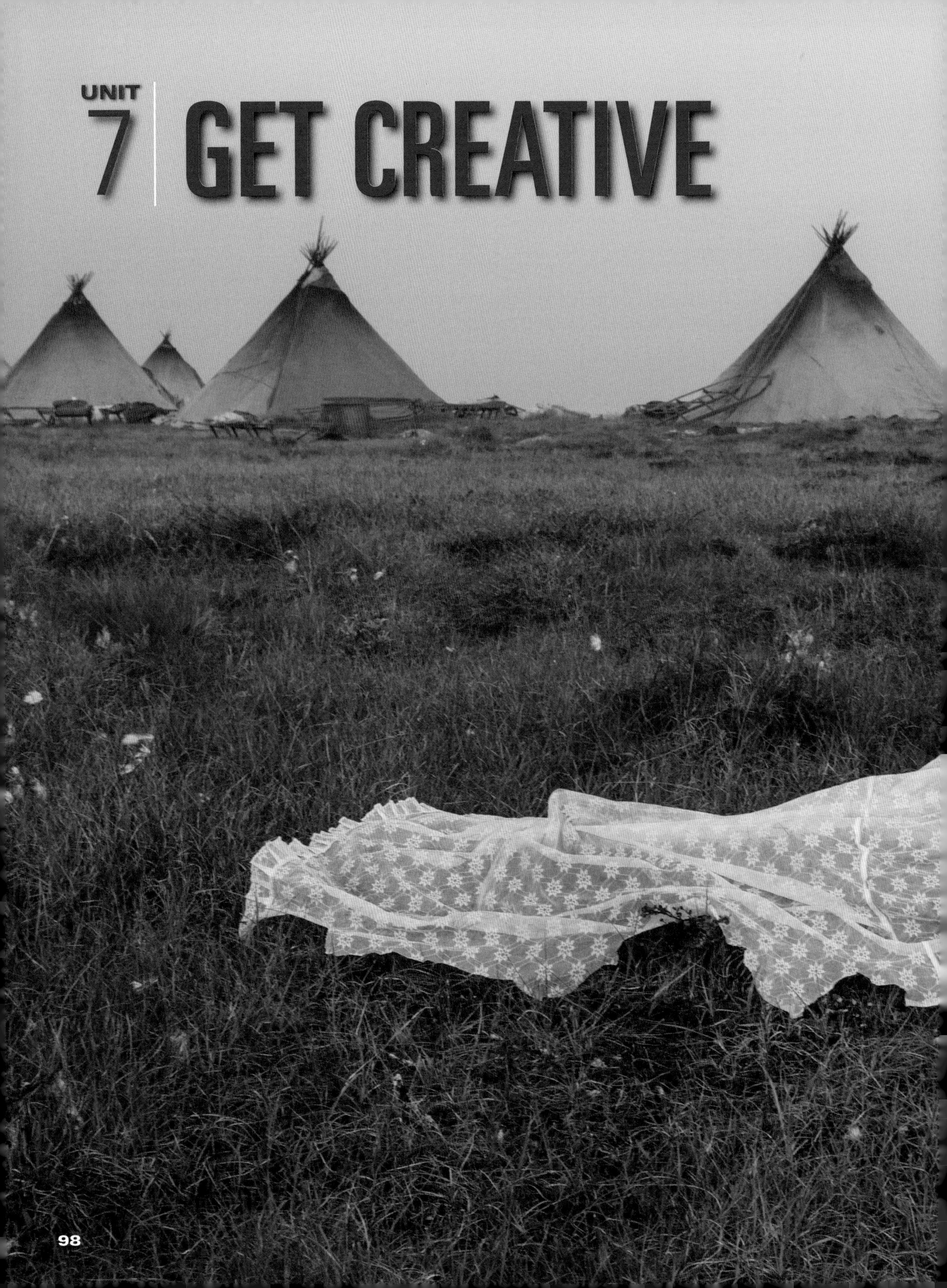

Wearing a curtain from a window and a crown she made from cardboard, a girl becomes the "tundra princess." Nenets camp near the Kara Sea in Siberia, Russia

IN THIS UNIT

▶ Discuss how boredom and creativity are related

▶ Question ideas about boredom

▶ Evaluate how personal habits affect creativity

▶ Present the results of a challenge to be more creative

SKILLS

LISTENING
Take notes: numbers and time periods

SPEAKING
Present results

GRAMMAR
-ing forms

CRITICAL THINKING
Question ideas

CONNECT TO THE TOPIC

1. How is the girl in the photo creative?
2. Do you think you are creative?

PREPARE TO WATCH

A VOCABULARY Listen to the words. Complete the sentences with the correct form of the words. Use a dictionary if necessary. ⏵7.1

decision (n)	generate (v)	occupied (adj)	previously (adv)	shock (v)
despite (prep)	obvious (adj)	participant (n)	report (v)	unpleasant (adj)

1. The students worked together to _____ some ideas for their final project.

2. My job and school work keep me _____ all day.

3. According to a study, 95 percent of college students _____ that their screen time is higher than they thought.

4. It was _____ the child had eaten the cookie. There were crumbs all over his face.

5. Be careful! If you touch the wire, you might _____ yourself.

6. I need to make a(n) _____ about my future. Do I work or go to college?

7. _____ her love of the phone game, she didn't play it for a week.

8. About 52% of the _____ in the study were women and 48% were men.

9. _____, teenagers owned fewer mobile phones than adults, but now the percentage who have a phone is about the same.

10. Most people think that being bored is a(n) _____ feeling.

A young woman passes time by playing a guitar.

B Listen to a pair of students discuss what they do when they are bored. Check (✓) the things the students mention. 🔊 7.2

☐ Check social media   ☐ Text people   ☐ Write in a journal
☐ Go shopping   ☐ Read a book   ☐ Eat
☐ Play an instrument   ☐ Watch TV   ☐ Exercise
☐ Listen to music   ☐ Draw or paint   ☐ Cook or bake

C **PERSONALIZE** Look at the list in activity B. Which of these things do you do when you are bored? Are there other things you do? Tell a partner.

D Listen again to the conversation from activity B. Write the missing filler words or phrases. 🔊 7.2

A: What do you do when you are bored?

B: ¹_____.
I usually look at my phone and check Twitter or Instagram. I used to read a lot, but I don't read as much now. How about you?

A: ²_____. I guess the same.
I check social media. I text my friends. I go to the gym a few times a week when I have time.

B: Do you ever do anything creative?

A: ³_____. Actually, yes. I write in my journal.
I write about my day, and sometimes I write poems or stories.

> **COMMUNICATION TIP**
>
> When you need a moment to think about an answer, you can use **filler words and phrases** to give yourself more time.
>
> *Hmm, let me see.*
>
> *Um, that's a good question.*
>
> *Let me think about that for a second.*

E Practice the conversation in activity D with a partner. Use filler words and your own ideas.

> A: *What do you do when you are bored?*
>
> B: *Hmm, let's see. I usually watch TV or listen to music.*

REFLECT   Discuss how boredom and creativity are related.

> You are going to watch a video that discusses research about boredom and creativity. Answer the questions with a partner or in a small group.
>
> 1. When do you usually feel bored?
> 2. When do you usually feel most creative?
> 3. Do you think that feeling bored and feeling creative are connected? Explain.

WHY BOREDOM IS **GOOD FOR YOU**

A PREDICT Watch the first part of the video. Then guess the percentage of women and men who shocked themselves rather than be bored? Fill in the bars on the graph. ▶ 7.1

Percent of People Who Shocked Themselves

100%
80%
60%
40%
20%
0%

Women   Men

B Watch the rest of the excerpt. Were your predictions close? Did the differences between women and men surprise you? ▶ 7.2

C PHRASES TO KNOW Work with a partner. Discuss the meaning of these phrases from the video. Then take turns answering the questions.

1. What do you think about when you let your **mind wander**?

2. What objects or things in your life do you need to **get rid of**?

D MAIN IDEAS Watch the complete video and choose the main ideas. ▶ 7.3

1. a. People would rather be bored than experience physical pain.

   b. People avoid being bored because it is unpleasant.

2. a. By avoiding boredom, you are able to be more creative.

   b. By avoiding boredom, you are likely making yourself less creative.

3. a. We can choose to allow ourselves to be bored or not.

   b. We cannot choose to allow ourselves to be bored or not.

E DETAILS Watch the video again. Choose the correct answers. ▶ 7.3

1. **17 / 70** percent of people spend some of their leisure time just sitting and thinking.

2. One way to avoid boredom is by **checking social media / sitting in a coffee shop.**

3. People are bored when **reading the news / waiting in line**.

4. Scientific research says we're **gaining / losing** something when we avoid boredom.

5. When you are bored, your **attention is focused / mind wanders**.

6. Research shows that mind wandering helps people be **more / less** creative.

7. Participants in a study were **more / less** creative after doing a boring task.

8. The student thinks that a phone **gets rid of / causes** boredom.

A chair in an empty room. How long could you sit in a room like this without anything to entertain you?

A woman uses plastic cups to grow plants.

F Form two groups. Do the plastic cup experiment from the video. Follow these steps.

1. Group 1: Do nothing for two minutes.

   Group 2: Look at your phone or book for two minutes.

2. Both groups: Write as many different uses for a plastic cup as you can think of.

3. As a class, discuss the results. Which group thought of more uses for the plastic cup?

G **NOTICE THE GRAMMAR** Underline the *-ing* words in the sentence starters below. What part of speech are they? Tell a partner. Then take turns completing the sentences with your own ideas.

1. Not having my phone with me makes me feel . . .

2. When I see an amazing animal or scene, I . . .

3. I'm interested in becoming . . .

GRAMMAR *-ing* forms

The present participle (*-ing* form of a verb) has two uses in addition to the present continuous.

Participial adjective: The *-ing* form can be used as an adjective. It can come before a noun or after a linking verb, such as *be*, *seem*, *look*, *sound*, or *appear*.

> *She had many creative and **interesting ideas**.* (adjective + noun)
> *The movie **looks boring**.* (linking verb + adjective)

Gerund: The *-ing* form can be used as a noun. A gerund can be a subject, an object of a verb, or an object of a preposition.

> *Sometimes, **forgetting** your phone is a good thing.* (subject)
> *I **considered giving up** video games for a few weeks.* (object of a verb)
> *I'm interested **in becoming** more creative.* (object of a preposition)

H GRAMMAR Complete the excerpt with the *-ing* form of one of the verbs. Then listen and check your answers. 🎧 7.3

avoid	be	bore	participate	relax	think	wander

Around 95 percent of American adults report ¹___participating___ in some leisure activities over the past 24 hours. But only 17 percent say they spent any time at all just ²_____ and ³_____, because that apparently is ⁴_____, and ⁵_____ bored is unpleasant. . . . But are we losing anything by ⁶_____ boredom? Well, scientific research says yes, and what we're losing is important. When you're bored, your mind wanders. That's only natural. The state of boredom is one where your attention is not focused on anything in particular. Researchers have shown this mind ⁷_____ is useful for creativity.

I Complete the sentences with the *-ing* form of the verb and your ideas. Then share your ideas with a partner.

1. The most _____ (bore) activity I regularly have to do is _____

   _____.

2. Three things I usually avoid _____ (do) are _____

   _____.

3. _____ (be) creative is important for my future because _____

   _____.

CRITICAL THINKING   Question ideas

When you read or hear about research, question the ideas presented. Consider your own experience, opposing ideas, and the source of the information.

REFLECT   Question ideas about boredom.

The video says that being bored is good for people and their creativity. Is this always true? Give an example of when boredom is not good. Then discuss your ideas with your class.

_____

_____

PREPARE TO LISTEN

Visitors at the Harvard Art Museum in Cambridge, Massachusetts, USA

A Discuss the questions with your class.

1. What are the people in the photo doing? What do you think about the situation?

2. How many times a day do you check your phone? Do you think you check it too many times? Not enough?

B **VOCABULARY** Listen to the words. Then complete the questions with the correct form of the words. Use a dictionary if necessary. 7.4

| challenge (n) | device (n) | notice (v) | restrict (v) | substantial (adj) |
| delete (v) | look at (v phr) | period (n) | shocking (adj) | usage (n) |

1. According to researchers, most young people spend a _____ amount of time on their phones. Do you think this is true?

2. The results of the experiment were _____. Can you believe that so many men would shock themselves to avoid being bored?

3. Why is it a good idea to _____ the amount of time you use your phone?

4. Have you ever tried a _____, such as exercising every day for a month?

5. Look around the room where you are now. Do you _____ anything new that you've never seen before? What is it?

6. Have you ever used an app to track your daily cell phone _____?

7. How often do you _____ old emails or text messages that you don't need anymore?

8. Have you ever _____ research related to social media?

9. Which electronic _____ do you use the most: a cell phone, a computer, or something else?

10. What time _____ in history do you think is the most interesting?

C PERSONALIZE Take turns answering the questions from activity B with a partner.

A: . . . Do you think this is true?

B: Maybe. My brother plays sports, so he doesn't spend as much time on his phone as other people I know.

REFLECT Evaluate how personal habits affect creativity.

You will listen to a radio show about phone usage and creativity. Look at the infographic. Tell a partner if you think the average hours of usage are correct. Then take turns answering the questions below.

Average Hours of Device Usage Per Day by Age Group

11.1 HOURS	9.6 HOURS	7.9 HOURS	6.1 HOURS	4.4 HOURS	OVERALL AVERAGE 7.8 HOURS
Teens (18–19)	Millenials (20–36)	Generation X (37–52)	Baby Boomers (53–70)	Over 71	

1. How many hours per week do people in your age group use a device? _____

2. How about in your parents' age group? _____

3. What is one way that a device can help people be more creative? _____
_____
_____

4. What is one way that a device might reduce creativity? _____
_____
_____

LISTEN & SPEAK

CHECKING IN AND CHECKING OUT

A PREDICT What do you think the radio show will say about phone usage and creativity? Tell a partner.

B PHRASES TO KNOW With your partner, discuss the meaning of these phrases from the radio show. Then take turns answering the questions.

1. How do you **stay in touch with** people from your past?

2. How long could you go without **checking in** on your phone?

3. What things do you do when you are relaxing or **checking out**?

4. Do you look at your phone a lot **out of habit**? What else do you do out of habit?

C Listen to the radio show and take notes in your notebook. Were your predictions from activity A correct? 🎧 7.5

D MAIN IDEAS Choose the two main ideas.

a. Research shows that the amount of time we spend on our cell phones is increasing.

b. In one study, college students spent an average of 277 minutes a day on their cell phones.

c. Challenges can help people control their phone usage.

LISTENING SKILL Take notes: numbers and time periods

As you listen, listen for numbers and time periods. These are often important details to remember. When taking notes, use abbreviations and symbols to write more quickly.

min = minutes	wk/wks = week(s)	yr/yrs = year(s)
1 min 30 mins	1 wk 2 wks	1 yr 5 yrs
hr/hrs = hour(s)	mo = month	/ = per
1 hr 3 hrs	1 mo 6 mos	3 days/wk

E DETAILS Listen to an excerpt from the radio show. Complete the notes about Rosen's research. Use the abbreviations and symbols from the Listening Skill box.  🎧 7.6

- ▸ Final yr of study, average daily screen time: ¹_____ / day.
- ▸ Over ²_____ day,
- ▸ 32 ³_____,
- ▸ Just over ⁴_____, and ⁵_____.

F DETAILS Listen to another excerpt. In your own words, write the challenge for each day. 🎧 7.7

Challenge one: _____

Challenge two: _____

Challenge three: _____.

Challenge four: _____

G Discuss the questions with a partner. Then choose one of the challenges and do it between now and the next class.

1. Which challenge would be the hardest for you? The easiest?
2. Which challenge will you do? Why did you choose it?

Highline athlete Thomas Spoettl takes a break
on an exposed highline in the Austrian Alps.

A radio show host

Present the results of a challenge to be more creative.

You are going to role-play a radio show with your group. You will take turns being the host while your group members call in and discuss the results of their challenges. Use the ideas, vocabulary, and skills from the unit.

H MODEL Listen to the callers discuss their challenges. Complete the chart. Discuss your answers with a partner and update your chart. 🎧 7.8

Name	Ritchie	Eva
Challenge #	3	
Reasons		
Results		
Plans for future		

PRONUNCIATION   Connected speech 🔊7.9

We often connect, or link, words. The end of one word connects with the beginning of the next word.

Final consonant to beginning vowel: When a word that begins with a vowel comes after a word ending in a consonant, the consonant sound often moves to the beginning of the next word.

> I **look at** my phone 15-20 **times a** day.

> I **loo kat** my phone 15-20 **time za** day.

Same consonants: We often omit the final consonant sound from the first word, and hold it a little longer.

> I deleted **both apps from my** phone.

> I deleted **bo thapps fro mmy** phone.

Final d + y: These two sounds often form the /dʒ/ sound, as in *just*.

> *Which challenge* **did you** *do?*

> *Which challenge* **di jou** *do?*

I   PRONUNCIATION Listen to an excerpt from the model. Complete the sentences with the phrases you hear. Listen again and read along. 🔊7.10

Radio Host: So, how ¹_____*did you*_____ feel? ²_____ notice?

Ritchie: Hmm. Good question… I was definitely ³_____ better mood

than usual ⁴_____ school. And then on the train, I had

⁵_____ about ⁶_____ write for a class assignment.

I think the time just sitting and thinking really helped me.

Radio Host: Has this experience ⁷_____ think about how your phone

affects your life? Will you ⁸_____ apps back to your phone?

Ritchie: Not right away. I ⁹_____ them off for a

¹⁰_____.

J   PRONUNCIATION Complete the sentences with your information. With a partner, ask and answer the questions. Use connected speech.

1. A: What challenge did you try?

    B: I tried challenge _____ because I hoped to _____.

2. A: What did you notice about yourself?

    B: I noticed I _____.

K PLAN Complete the chart with the results of your challenge.

Challenge #	
Reasons	
Results	
Plans for future	

SPEAKING SKILL   Present results

When you are talking about the results of an experiment or other experience:

▸ Say what the experiment (or challenge) was and the reason for it.
   I chose challenge . . . because . . .
   I wanted to find out . . .

▸ Give the results or tell what happened.
   I found that. . . .

▸ Focus on the most important or most surprising results.
   I was surprised that . . .
   It was interesting that . . .

▸ Give a conclusion and say what the results mean for the future.
   I believe the results show/mean that . . .
   The results seem to suggest that . . .

L APPLY In a small group, present the results of your challenge.

M UNIT TASK Present your radio show to another group or the class. As you listen, take notes about another group. Did you notice any similarities?

Name			
Challenge #			
Reasons			
Results			
Plans for future			

REFLECT

A Check (✓) the Reflect activities you can do and the academic skills you can use.

☐ discuss how boredom and creativity are related

☐ question ideas about boredom

☐ evaluate how personal habits affect creativity

☐ present the results of a challenge to be more creative

☐ take notes: numbers and time periods

☐ present results

☐ *-ing* forms

☐ question ideas

B Write the vocabulary words from the unit in the correct column. Add any other words that you learned. Circle words you still need to practice.

NOUN	VERB	ADJECTIVE	ADVERB & OTHER

C Reflect on the ideas in the unit as you answer these questions.

1. What steps will you take to become more creative?

_____

_____

_____

2. What ideas or skills in this unit will be most useful to you in the future?

_____

_____

_____

UNIT

8 | IS THERE GOOD IN GAMING?

Team Fnatic, left, and Invictus
Gaming compete on stage
during the League of Legends
World Championship Finals in
Incheon, South Korea.

CONNECT TO THE TOPIC

1. Describe the photo. How does it make you feel?
2. Who do you think plays the most video games?

PREPARE TO LISTEN

A VOCABULARY Listen to the words. Match the words with the definitions. Use a dictionary if necessary. 🎧 8.1

1. _____ addicted (adj)   a. not very important or large

2. _____ come out (v phr)   b. if

3. _____ common (adj)   c. the belief that you can do things well

4. _____ confidence (n)   d. unable to stop doing something

5. _____ cooperate (v)   e. something that isn't good or causes problems

6. _____ disadvantage (n)   f. a feeling about something

7. _____ ignore (v)   g. to work with one or more people to achieve a result

8. _____ sense (n)   h. to not pay attention to someone or something

9. _____ trivial (adj)   i. ordinary or usual

10. _____ whether (conj)   j. to become available to buy or use

B VOCABULARY Complete the conversation with the correct form of the words from activity A. Then listen and check your answers. 🎧 8.2

Student: Did you join any clubs when you were a student, Professor King?

Professor: Yes, I was in the computer club. Why do you ask?

Student: I'm thinking about joining a video-gaming team, but I don't know ¹_____ it's a good idea. I'm really busy with class assignments.

Professor: I think you should do it. Being on a team is a great way to develop certain skills. For example, you have to work with your teammates, so you learn how to ²_____ with others. Also, winning a competition can give you a strong ³_____ of success. And it can help build your ⁴_____ and make you feel good about yourself.

Student: Those are all good points, but I don't know if I have time.

Professor: Do you spend any time with friends?

Student: No, I'm always studying.

Professor: You need to spend time with friends. It's great to work hard, but don't ⁵_____ your social life. You also have to have some fun!

Student: Thanks, Professor. I think I'll give it a try.

The winning debate team poses for a photo at City University of Hong Kong.

C Discuss the questions with a partner.

1. What are some **common** reasons that people like to join clubs or teams?

2. How can joining a club or team help with a person's **confidence**?

3. Do you think a person can be **addicted** to technology, such as smartphones or online games? Explain.

When someone asks you a *yes/no* question, it's a good idea to add information after *yes* or *no* to **keep the conversation going**.

    A: *Do you play video games?*

    B: *Yes, **I play for about an hour a day**.*

D Find and underline two examples of *yes* or *no* with additional information in the conversation in activity B.

E Take turns asking and answering the questions with a partner. Use *yes* or *no* with additional information in your answers.

1. Are there any hobbies or sports that you like?

2. Have you played many video games?

3. Do you think playing video games is good for you?

REFLECT   Consider reasons for joining a club or team.

Before you listen to a podcast about the effects of participating in online gaming, discuss the questions with a partner.

1. Think about an activity you participate in. Why do you participate in it?

2. Think about an activity you do not participate in? Why don't you participate in it?

EFFECTS OF ONLINE GAMING

Players Gabi and Showliana during the Girl Gamer Brazil festival in São Paulo, Brazil

A PREDICT Listen to the first part of an interview with a psychologist. What do you think the psychologist will say about video games? Choose your answer. 🎧8.3

   a. They are good for us.

   b. They are bad for us.

   c. They are good and bad for us.

B PHRASES TO KNOW Work with a partner. Discuss the meaning of these phrases from the podcast. Then take turns answering the questions.

   1. Do you know anyone whose hobby **takes control of** his or her life? Explain.

   2. Do you think **social skills** are as important as other skills? Explain.

   3. **For the most part**, do your friends use text messages, phone calls, or email to communicate?

C MAIN IDEAS Listen to the podcast. Choose the two main ideas. 🎧8.4

   a. Playing video games can be harmful to a small group of people.

   b. Video games are becoming more challenging to play.

   c. There are a lot of benefits to playing video games with other people.

   d. Some video games are for groups of players.

   e. Video games are often bad for young people.

LISTENING SKILL   Use a T-chart to take notes

When you listen to someone compare two things, you can take notes in a T-chart. This will help you organize the ideas. For example, you can use a T-chart to note the pros and cons of an activity.

Pros of joining a club	Cons of joining a club
- meet new people	- takes a lot of time

D DETAILS Listen again. Complete the notes in the chart. 🎧8.4

Cons of playing video games	Pros of playing video games

▸ some gamers are unhealthy
  • don't [1] _exercise_
  • eat junk food
▸ some are anti-social
  • no [2] _____
▸ some ignore important things
  • school, work, [3] _____
▸ some are [4] _____ but a trivial number
	▸ games can develop [5] _____ skills
	  • find [6] _____ to problems
	    • make [7] _____ decisions
	    • follow instructions
	    • develop [8] _____
	▸ better [9] _____ skills
	  • strong sense of [10] _____
	  • more [11] _____
	  • [12] _____ loneliness

> **CRITICAL THINKING** Evaluate pros and cons
>
> Some pros and cons are more important than others because they affect a lot of people while others do not. Learning how to evaluate them is useful when you organize ideas for presentations or essays. Focus on the more important pros or cons in your speaking or writing.

E APPLY Look at the chart in activity D. Check (✓) the pros and cons that you think are most important. Explain your reasons to a partner

F Answer the questions with a partner.

1. Do you play video games? If yes, which kind do you play: MMOs or single player? If no, which type sounds more interesting?

2. Look at the list of pros in activity D. What other activities have the same pros?

G NOTICE THE GRAMMAR Match the sentence beginnings (1–3) with their endings (a–c). Which part of each sentence describes a purpose or a reason? Tell a partner.

1. To help us find out the truth, _____

2. To prepare for a competition, _____

3. Gamers must cooperate with a lot of other players _____

a. in order to play successfully.

b. players practice daily.

c. we have psychologist Dr. Jennifer Lee with us today.

GRAMMAR Infinitives of purpose

An **infinitive of purpose** answers the question "Why?" and has the form *to* + base verb or *in order to* + base verb. It explains the reason for some action. The infinitive of purpose can go at the beginning or the end of a sentence. *In order to* is more formal.

> ***To reach*** *the next level of the game, you have to get five points.*
> ***In order to reach*** *the next level of the game, you have to get five points.*

> *You have to get five points* ***(in order) to reach*** *the next level of the game.*
> *Some people play video games* ***(in order) to exercise*** *their brains.*

For the negative, use *in order not to* + verb.

> ***In order not to lose*** *the game, you have to stay on your side.*
> *You have to stay on your side* ***in order not to lose*** *the game.*

Professional esports players celebrating a win

H GRAMMAR Complete the sentences with infinitives of purpose.

help	learn	meet	reach	show	win

1. _____ the championships, the team had to win several competitions.

2. Eri decided to join a club at school _____ new people.

3. After the team won, they took their coach out to dinner _____ their appreciation.

4. _____ a game, a player must be able to think more quickly than the other player.

5. She watched a few videos _____ how to play the game.

6. Doctors sometimes use video games _____ patients recover from injuries.

I GRAMMAR Complete the sentences with your own ideas. Use infinitives of purpose.

1. I'm taking this class _____.

2. Many people play video games _____.

3. I think people play team sports _____.

4. I believe people join clubs _____.

5. I'd like to get a job as a _____ _____.

REFLECT Evaluate your attitude toward video gaming.

Answer the questions with a partner or in a small group.

1. Do you have a mostly positive or negative attitude toward video gaming as a social activity? Explain.

2. Have your views changed about video games?

PREPARE TO WATCH

A VOCABULARY Listen to the words. Complete the sentences with the correct form of the words. Use a dictionary if necessary. 🎧 8.5

accompany (v)	approximately (adv)	compete (v)	look into (v phr)	remain (v)
animation (n)	audience (n)	cooperative (adj)	mate (n)	transport (v)

1. I need to _____ the effects of video gaming for my project, so I'm going to learn how to play a few.

2. At video game conventions, gamers _____ against each other for prizes.

3. Everyone in our group was _____, so we finished the project without any problems.

4. The male bird sings to attract a _____.

5. We need a big truck to _____ all of the company's computer equipment.

6. If you don't want to go to the computer repair store alone, I can _____ you.

7. Some games are created for a specific _____, such as people who love sports.

8. According to a recent study, _____ 35 percent of video game players are 21 to 35 years old.

9. Many people _____ in their hometowns their whole lives.

10. There are many free software programs that help you create _____.

B VOCABULARY Work with a partner. Choose the best meaning for each word.

1. If you **accompany** someone, you _____ them.
    a. go with   b. call   c. remember

2. **Approximately** 25 percent means _____ 25 percent.
    a. exactly   b. about   c. more than

3. An **audience** is a group of people who _____.
    a. work together   b. play a sport   c. watch or use something

4. When you **compete** in an activity, you try to _____.
    a. have fun   b. win   c. meet people

5. When you make an **animation**, you make _____.
    a. a movie with real people   b. a photo   c. a drawing that moves

6. When you are **cooperative**, you are _____ to work with.
    a. easy   b. fun   c. interesting

7. If a female spider is looking for a **mate**, it is looking for _____.

    a. a place to make a web   b. a male spider   c. an insect to eat

8. If you **look into** something, you _____ it.

    a. find out about   b. explain   c. create

9. If you **remain** in a place, you _____.

    a. move there   b. stay there   c. explore it

10. If you **transport** something, you _____ it.

    a. manage   b. buy   c. move

C PERSONALIZE Discuss the questions with a partner.

1. Do you enjoy **competing** with other people? Explain.

2. Are there any places you will go only if someone **accompanies** you?

3. What is your primary mode of **transport**: car, bike, or some other vehicle?

D Study the infographic. Then discuss the questions below with a partner.

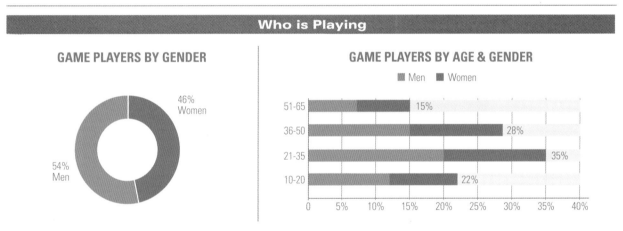

Note: the data varies according to the type of video game.

1. What does the infographic show?

2. Read the note. Do you think men and women like different kinds of video games?

3. Do you think people in different age groups like different kinds of video games?

REFLECT Discuss players and types of video games.

You are going to watch a video about a different type of video game company. Discuss these questions with a partner.

1. Does anything in the infographic surprise you? Explain.

2. Do you think video games can teach people? Explain.

3. What types of video games most appeal to you? If none do, explain why.

GAMING FOR GOOD

A young orangutan
swings in the trees in
Kalimantan, Indonesia.

A PREDICT You will watch a video about National Geographic Explorer Gautam Shah's
video game company, Internet of Elephants. Look at the photo and read the caption. What
type of video games do you think Shah's company creates?

B PHRASES TO KNOW With a partner, discuss the meaning of these phrases from the video. Then take turns answering the questions.

1. Have you ever **gone outside of your comfort zone**? If so, what happened?

2. Do animals and nature **play a big part** in your life? Explain.

3. How do movies and TV shows **bring** history **to life**?

C MAIN IDEAS Watch the video. Why does Gautam Shah make video games? ▶ 8.1

a. To follow animals and learn about their lives and habits

b. To help people take better photographs of nature and animals

c. To make people care about and protect wild animals

D DETAILS Watch the video again. Write T for *True*, F for *False*, or NG for *Not Given*. ▶ 8.1

1. _____ Shah uses fake data for his games and programs.

2. _____ Shah used GPS data to create an animation about a real lion.

3. _____ Shah's games earn money for wildlife conservation.

4. _____ In *Wildeverse*, players can find wild animals in their own cities.

5. _____ The animals in *Wildeverse* are based on real animals in the wild.

6. _____ *Wildeverse* players earn points for finding animals.

E Look at the information from the *Wildeverse* website about Fio the orangutan. Discuss the questions in a small group.

1. What kind of information does the website provide about Fio?

2. Why do you think it gives this information?

3. How does it make you feel about Fio?

FIO THE BORNEAN ORANGUTAN

Gender: Female

Home: Sebangau National Park
Central Kalimantan, Indonesia

Age: 7

Personality: As a younger orangutan, Fio was extremely social and playful. She even played with Chilli the gibbon (very unusual). She is used to researchers, as they have followed her around since she was a baby.

You are going to review a video game or an app. You will explain how it works, describe its pros and cons, and make a conclusion about it. Use the ideas, vocabulary, and skills from the unit.

F MODEL Listen to the review of a game. Complete the chart. Discuss your answers with a partner and update your chart. 🎧 8.6

Game or app	Wildeverse
Description	
Pros	
Cons	
Conclusion	

A player of Wildeverse finds an orangutan in a virtual tree.

PRONUNCIATION   Thought groups 🎧 8.7

In writing, we use commas and other punctuation to express our thoughts clearly. When speaking, we use pauses to divide sentences into thought groups. A thought group expresses a single thought.

A: *After joining the team, / she seemed happier.*
B: *Really? / Why do you think that?*
A: *I'm not sure. / I guess / because she's made new friends.*

Here are some examples of common thought groups.

Short statements	Prepositional phrases	Clauses	Set phrases
I don't know.	*In this game,*	*After the game is over,*	*What I mean is*
I think so.	*For example,*	*When I see you again,*	*On one hand,*
Thank you very much.	*In addition,*	*. . . so they learn a lot*	*On the other hand,*

G PRONUNCIATION Choose the sentence with the correct thought groups. Then listen and check your answers. Listen again and read the correct sentence with the speaker. 🎧 8.8

1. a. The animals that / players see are / actually real animals who / live in the wild.

    b. The animals that players see / are actually real animals / who live in the wild.

2. a. When they take photos of the animals, / players learn information about them, / such as where they live / and what their personalities are like.

    b. When they take photos / of the animals, players learn information about them, / such as where they live and / what their personalities are like.

3. a. *Wildeverse* is fun to play, / but it also has a lot of benefits.

    b. *Wildeverse* is fun / to play, but it also has / a lot of benefits.

4. a. For example, players / often feel like / part of a community.

    b. For example, / players often feel like part of a community.

5. a. Also, players / walk around to find / the animals, so they get exercise while / they play.

    b. Also, / players walk around to find the animals, / so they get exercise / while they play.

SPEAKING SKILL   Use signal words and phrases

You can use signal words and phrases to let the listener know what kind of information you are about to share. Here are some signal words and phrases for:

Giving an example: *For example, For instance*
Adding information: *Also, In addition, Finally*
Comparing or contrasting information: *Similarly, However*
Concluding a presentation: *In conclusion, In summary*

H APPLY Choose the correct signal words. Then listen to the excerpt from the model and check your answers. 🎧 8.9

The game has several pros. [1] **For example / Finally / Similarly**, players can share photos with other players from around the world, so they become part of a community. [2] **However / In addition / In summary**, *Wildeverse* encourages players to go outside and explore their neighborhoods. [3] **For example / Finally / Similarly**, the game helps with animal conservation. The money that players pay goes to conservation organizations. Learning about the wild animals and their problems may make players more interested in helping protect them.

The game also has a few cons. Because the game is new, there aren't very many animals yet. [4] **Also / For example / However**, there is only a little information about the animals.

[5] **For instance / Similarly / In conclusion**, even though *Wildeverse* has a couple of cons, I think it's a great game. . . .

I APPLY Complete parts of a review with signal words. More than one answer is possible.

1. The game has many pros. _____, it is easy to learn. _____, there are a lot of players, so you can meet people from around the world. _____, you can learn about the world as you play.

2. I really like the game. _____, it has a few cons . . .

3. _____, this game is great. It has a few issues, but it is easy to play. If you like wild animals and video games, I suggest you give it a try.

J PLAN Choose a video game or an app for your review. Complete the chart.

Game or app	
Description	
Pros	
Cons	
Conclusion	

K UNIT TASK Present your review in a group. Take notes in a chart in your notebook for each presentation. Which game or app sounds the most fun or useful to you?

REFLECT

A Check (✓) the Reflect activities you can do and the academic skills you can use.

☐ consider reasons for joining a club or team   ☐ use a T-chart to take notes

☐ evaluate your attitude toward video gaming   ☐ use signal words and phrases

☐ discuss players and types of video games   ☐ infinitives of purpose

☐ present a review of a video game or an app   ☐ evaluate pros and cons

B Write the vocabulary words from the unit in the correct column. Add any other words that you learned. Circle words you still need to practice.

NOUN	VERB	ADJECTIVE	ADVERB & OTHER

C Reflect on the ideas in the unit as you answer these questions.

1. How has the information from the unit changed or supported your opinion of video games?

_____

_____

_____

2. What ideas or skills in this unit will be most useful to you in the future?

_____

_____

_____

Suffix -ion

Suffixes come at the end of words. You can add the suffix -ion to some verbs to make abstract nouns. If a verb ends in -ate or -ute, remove the -e.

> construct + **ion** = construct**ion**
> donate + **ion** = dona**tion**

A Complete each sentence with a noun. Use the verbs in the box and -ion. Two words are extra.

act	attract	connect	contribute
donate	obligate	pollute	populate

1. By 2050, the _____ on Earth may be over ten billion people.

2. Social media sites are a popular way for people to make _____ s with old friends.

3. The _____ of each neighbor can make community events more enjoyable.

4. City leaders have a(n) _____ to make sure their communities are safe.

5. Many charities accept _____ s of clothes, books, and money.

6. The police often take _____ when people complain about noisy neighbors.

Using a dictionary   Example sentences

In addition to a definition, dictionaries will usually show a word in an example sentence. You can use the example sentence to better understand how the word is used. An example sentence also gives clues to the words that collocate (or go) with the target word.

> issue /ˈɪʃu/ v [T] **-sued, -suing, -sues 1** to give or send out: *Between 1941 and 1945, the White House issued news about the war nearly every day.* **2** to give or provide in a formal or official way: *The motor vehicle office issues drivers' licenses after people pass a test.*

B Use a dictionary. Write an example sentence for each word. Use the definition from Unit 1.

1. actual: _____

2. generous: _____

3. impossible: _____

4. positive: _____

5. support: _____

Formal and informal language

In professional or academic settings—such as in a presentation—you are likely to use formal language. In casual conversation or more personal settings, you often use less formal language. The words you choose can show this difference.

More formal: *She **regretted** her mistake.*

More informal: *She **was sorry about** her mistake.*

Notice that in formal language, you may use longer, single words than in informal language. You also don't use spoken expressions and phrases such as "sorry about" as often.

A Match the formal word with the correct informal word or phrase. Check your answers in a dictionary.

More formal	More informal
1. author _____	a. say
2. elderly _____	b. really big
3. inadequate _____	c. writer
4. mention _____	d. older
5. immense _____	e. not enough

Prefixes *in-*, *im-*, and *mis-*

Prefixes come at the beginning of words. You can add a prefix to a word to change its meaning. You can add the prefixes *in-*, *im-*, and *mis-* to some adjectives and verbs to give them the opposite meaning.

***in** + expensive = **in**expensive*, meaning "not expensive"

Look in a dictionary to check for the correct spelling.

B Choose the correct prefix *in, im,* or *mis* to make the opposite meaning of the words. Write the words. Use a dictionary if necessary.

1. attentive: _____

2. patient: _____

3. adequate: _____

4. understand: _____

5. probable: _____

6. heard: _____

Suffixes Change nouns and verbs to adjectives

A suffix comes at the end of a word. Some suffixes can change adjectives into nouns or verbs.

Common suffixes for adjectives are: *-able, -ed, -ic, -ing,* and *-ish.*

Words that end in *-ing* and *-ed* can be adjectives or verb forms. Use the context to decide if the word is an adjective or verb.

A Choose the correct adjective form for each noun or verb. Use a dictionary if necessary.

1. fool   a. fooling   b. foolish   c. fooly

2. publish   a. publisher   b. publishing   c. publishable

3. rely   a. reliable   b. relic   c. relied

4. convince   a. convincer   b. convincing   c. convincish

5. symbol   a. symbolic   b. symbolize   c. symbolly

Using a dictionary Choose the correct meaning

Many words have two or more meanings. In a dictionary, each word entry uses a numbered list to show the different definitions. For example, there are three main meanings for the verb *spread*. In Unit 3, the second definition is used for *spread*.

spread (v) **1** to cover a surface **2** to cause to go to many people **3** to lay out flat

B Use a dictionary. For each word below, find the best definition about the topic of "news." Write the definition.

1. article (n) _____

2. bulletin (v) _____

3. report (v) _____

4. paper (n) _____

5. media (adj) _____

Polysemy Multiple-meaning words

Polysemy refers to a word that has two or more different meanings. Sometimes the meanings are similar but not exactly the same.

> *She never goes out in **public**.* (the area outside one's home)
> *The law doesn't have **public** support.* (the people of a local area)

Use context clues—the words before and after a word—to help you decide which is the correct meaning of a word with polysemy.

A Choose the best meaning for the words in bold. Use context clues to help.

1. He **entertained** the idea of watching the news. But then he decided to watch a movie instead.

   a. to amuse   b. to consider   c. to give parties

2. His glasses **reflected** the clouds in the sky.

   a. to show an image of   b. to think about   c. to give off shine

3. She was a scientist. Then she went in a different **direction** and became an artist.

   a. geographical movement   b. new action   c. leadership

4. They **removed** all the furniture before painting the room.

   a. to move something away b. to get rid of   c. to make someone leave

Word families Nouns, verbs, and adjectives

You can add a suffix to some verbs to change them to nouns and adjectives.

Common suffixes for nouns are: *-ion, -ation,* and *-ment.*
Common suffixes for adjectives are: *-ed, -ible, -ing,* and *-ive.*

Some words can be both nouns and verbs, and their spelling does not change.

*I **work** at a supermarket. It's hard **work**.*
  verb   noun

B Complete the chart with the correct noun and adjective forms. Use a dictionary if necessary.

Noun	Verb	Adjective
	access	
	connect	
	entertain	
	expect	
	support	

Suffixes -er , -or, and -ant

You can add the suffixes -er , -or, and -ant to some verbs to make nouns. These suffixes often mean "a person or thing that does something."

> play + **er** = play**er**, a noun meaning "someone who *plays* a game."

A Complete each sentence with the correct noun form. Use a verb in the box and -er , -or, or -ant. One word is extra. Check your spelling in a dictionary.

act	apply	assist	contest	rescue	survive

1. Someone who saves people is a(n) _____.

2. Someone whose job is to help is a(n) _____.

3. Someone who lives after a difficult experience is a(n) _____.

4. Someone who takes part in a competition is a(n) _____.

5. Someone who performs in a movie or play is a(n) _____.

Polysemy Multiple-meaning words

Polysemy refers to a word that has two or more different meanings. Sometimes the meanings are similar but not exactly the same.

For example, the noun *head* can mean "a person in charge" or "the body part above your neck." Use context clues—the words before and after a word—to help you choose the correct meaning.

B Choose the best meaning of the words in bold. Use context clues to help. Check your answers in a dictionary.

1. Baseball players stay **alert** during a game. They don't want to get hit by the ball.

   a. alarm or sign of danger   b. attentive

2. The police detective cleverly **trapped** the criminal into confessing his crime.

   a. to catch or trick   b. to separate out

3. The party was a **disaster**—no one came!

   a. a total failure   b. an act of destruction

4. That was a **sick** joke to play on your brother.

   a. not healthy   b. very unkind

5. NASA's **mission** is to explore space.

   a. a purpose   b. a group sent to negotiate with another country

Word roots *psych, syn/sym,* and *situ*

Many words in English are formed from Latin and Greek word roots. Knowing the meaning of these word roots can help you understand the meaning of unfamiliar vocabulary.

The word root *psych* comes from Greek and means "mind."
The word root *syn* or *sym* comes from Greek and means "together."
The root word *situ* means "place" in Latin.

A Read the sentences and answer the questions about the words in bold. Then check your answers in a dictionary.

1. A **psychiatrist** at the hospital said the patient was unwell. What does a **psychiatrist** do?

   _____

2. The **psychic** looked at the customer and could see into her future? What ability does a **psychic** have? _____

3. The **campsite** was flooded, so we had to find a hotel. What is a **campsite**?

   _____

4. Only the violinist is here! It's hard to play a **symphony** with just one violinist. What is a **symphony**? _____

5. The song is a **synthesis** of many different styles—rap, rock, and country. What do you do when you **synthesize** things? _____

Frayer model

You can better learn new words and phrases by using a Frayer Model. A Frayer Model is a graphic organizer that helps you describe a word in more detail than just with a definition.

Defintion	Important characteristics
A diet is a weight loss program.	Avoid eating foods that cause weight gain. Usually focused on avoiding fats and sugars. Usually lasts for a few months or longer
a diet	
Examples	Non-examples
The Paleo diet, Vegan diet, vegetaran diet, low-fat diet	Fatty foods, fast foods, candy, sodas

B In your notebook, complete two Frayer Models for the words *relationship* and *painful*.

Using a dictionary Synonyms

Synonyms are words that are very similar in meaning. The words *large* and *big* are synonyms. A dictionary may include synonyms for common words. These words may be set in a box labeled *Thesaurus* or marked with the *SYN*. You can also look for synonyms in a thesaurus.

THESAURUS
trash (n) garbage, junk, rubbish, litter

A Use a dictionary. Match each word with the correct synonym.

1. average (adj) _____   a. noticeable

2. challenge (n) _____   b. attempt

3. effort (n) _____   c. test

4. notice (v) _____   d. everyday

5. obvious (adj) _____   e. become aware of

Collocations *Make* and *do* + noun

Collocations are two or more words that often go together. It is useful to learn collocations in the same way you learn an individual word.

The verbs *do* and *make* collocate with particular nouns. For example, you can *make a comment,* but you can't *do a comment.*

do	*make*
research	decisions
homework	a choice
chores	an effort
exercise	a report
nothing	speeches

B Complete the sentences using the correct form of the collocations from the box above. More than one answer may be possible.

1. Politicians often _____ that are very long.

2. It is hard to _____ about the future.

3. Scientists often _____ in a lab.

4. Many parents ask their children to _____ around the house.

5. It is hard to _____ when you are really tired.

Using a dictionary Antonyms

Antonyms are words that are opposite in meaning. The words *tall* and *short* are antonyms. Use a dictionary to find antonyms for common words. Antonyms are often labeled *ANT* or *OPP*, meaning "opposite." They may be listed after a definition for the word or in a *Thesaurus* box near the word. You can also look for antonyms in a thesaurus.

THESAURUS
tall (adj) high. *Ant.* short.

A Use a dictionary. Match each word with the correct antonym.

1. tense _____   a. notice

2. common _____   b. unsure

3. ignore _____   c. leave

4. remain _____   d. relaxed

5. confident _____   e. rare

Phrasal verbs with *look*

A phrasal verb is a two- or three-part verb phrase. It always contains one verb and at least one other small word called a "particle." The meaning of some phrasal verbs is easy to guess—for example, *get up,* means "to get out of bed." The meaning of other phrasal verbs is less obvious—for example *show up* means "to arrive where someone is waiting." Use context to help you understand the correct meaning.

> **look after:** *to keep someone or something in good condition*
> **look back:** *to think about things that happened in the past*
> **look forward to:** *to get excited about a future event*
> **look into:** *to find out about something*
> **look through:** *to get an idea about a written document by reading parts of it*
> **look up to:** *to respect or admire someone*

C Underline the phrasal verbs in these questions. Then answer the questions.

1. What is something you are looking forward to? _____

2. What was the last magazine you looked through? _____

3. Who do you look up to? _____

4. Looking back, what's the bravest thing you've done? _____

_____

5. Who looks after you, or who do you look after? _____

VOCABULARY INDEX

Unit 1	Page	CEFR
actual	10	B2
appear	10	B1
atmosphere	4	B1
average	4	B1
discover	4	B1
donation	10	B2
event	10	B1
generous	10	B1
impossible	10	B1
issue*	10	B1
obligation	4	B2
opportunity	4	B1
participate*	10	B2
population	4	B1
positive*	10	B2
stable*	4	C1
support	10	B1
trust	4	B1
unique*	4	B2
whenever	4	B1

Unit 2	Page	CEFR
according to	20	B1
appearance	26	B1
attention	20	B1
author*	20	B1
background	20	B1
contain	26	B1
distinct*	26	C1
diversity*	26	C1
document*	26	B1
elder	26	B1
expand*	26	B2
field	20	B2
immense	26	C1
inadequate*	26	C1
mention	20	B1
misunderstanding	20	B2
patient	20	B1
speech	20	B1
value	26	B1
widespread*	20	C1

Unit 3	Page	CEFR
article	36	B1
aware*	42	B2
common sense	42	B1
convince*	36	B1
evaluate*	36	C1
fool	36	B2
indicate*	42	B2
journalist	42	B1
professional*	42	B2
publish*	42	B1
purpose	36	B1
recognize	36	B2
reliable*	36	B2
result	36	B1
seem	42	B1
source*	36	B2
spread	42	B2
symbol*	42	B2
the media*	36	B2
well-known	42	B2

Unit 4	Page	CEFR
accessible*	52	B2
appreciate*	58	B2
definitely*	58	B1
direction	58	B1
emotional	58	B2
entertain	58	B1
essential	58	B1
expect	52	B1
express	52	B2
image*	58	B2
imagination	58	B1
influence	58	B2
motivation*	52	B2
passionate	58	B2
process*	52	B2
public	52	B1
reflect	52	B2
remove*	52	B1
society	52	B1
temporary*	52	B1

*Academic words

VOCABULARY INDEX

IRREGULAR VERB FORMS

Base form	Simple past	Past participle	Base form	Simple past	Past participle
be	was, were	been	lay	laid	laid
beat	beat	beaten	lead	led	led
become	became	become	leave	left	left
begin	began	begun	lend	lent	lent
bend	bent	bent	let	let	let
bite	bit	bitten	lie	lay	lain
blow	blew	blown	light	lit/lighted	lit/lighted
break	broke	broken	lose	lost	lost
bring	brought	brought	make	made	made
build	built	built	mean	meant	meant
buy	bought	bought	meet	met	met
catch	caught	caught	pay	paid	paid
choose	chose	chosen	prove	proved	proved/proven
come	came	come	put	put	put
cost	cost	cost	quit	quit	quit
cut	cut	cut	read	read	read
dig	dug	dug	ride	rode	ridden
dive	dived/dove	dived	ring	rang	rung
do	did	done	rise	rose	risen
draw	drew	drawn	run	ran	run
drink	drank	drunk	say	said	said
drive	drove	driven	sit	sat	sat
eat	ate	eaten	sleep	slept	slept
fall	fell	fallen	slide	slid	slid
feed	fed	fed	speak	spoke	spoken
feel	felt	felt	spend	spent	spent
fight	fought	fought	spread	spread	spread
find	found	found	stand	stood	stood
fit	fit	fit/fitted	steal	stole	stolen
fly	flew	flown	stick	stuck	stuck
forget	forgot	forgotten	strike	struck	struck
forgive	forgave	forgiven	swear	swore	sworn
freeze	froze	frozen	sweep	swept	swept
get	got	got/gotten	swim	swam	swum
give	gave	given	take	took	taken
go	went	gone	teach	taught	taught
grow	grew	grown	tear	tore	torn
hang	hung	hung	tell	told	told
have	had	had	think	thought	thought
hear	heard	heard	throw	threw	thrown
hide	hid	hidden	understand	understood	understood
hit	hit	hit	upset	upset	upset
hold	held	held	wake	woke	woken
hurt	hurt	hurt	wear	wore	worn
keep	kept	kept	win	won	won
know	knew	known	write	wrote	written

SOUNDS & SYMBOLS

Vowel sounds

1. **e**at, sl**ee**p /iʸ/
2. **i**t, s**i**p /ɪ/
3. l**a**te, r**ai**n /eʸ/
4. w**e**t, p**e**n /ɛ/
5. c**a**t, f**a**n /æ/
6. b**i**rd, t**u**rn /ɜr/
7. c**u**t, s**u**n /ʌ/
   about, b**e**fore /ə/ (schwa)
8. n**o**t, t**o**p /ɑ/
9. t**oo**, f**ew** /uʷ/
10. g**oo**d, sh**ou**ld /ʊ/
11. t**oe**, n**o** /oʷ/
12. s**aw**, w**a**lk /ɔ/

Dipthongs
13. f**i**ne, r**i**ce /ay/
14. **ou**t, n**ow** /aw/
15. b**oy**, j**oi**n /ɔy/

Consonant sounds

1. **p**en /p/
2. **b**ag /b/

3. **t**ime /t/
4. **d**og /d/

5. **k**eep /k/
6. **g**et /g/

7. **f**eel /f/
8. **v**ery /v/

9. **th**in /θ/
10. **th**e /ð/

11. **s**ale /s/
12. ea**s**y, cau**s**e /z/
13. **sh**e /ʃ/
14. trea**s**ure /ʒ/
15. **ch**icken /tʃ/
16. **j**oin /dʒ/

17. **m**e /m/
18. **n**ot /n/
19. ri**ng** /ŋ/

20. **l**ose /l/
21. **r**ead, **wr**ite /r/

22. **w**in /w/
23. **y**ou /y/
24. **h**ome /h/

COMMON TERMS

syllable: a unit of sound; one or more syllables make a word. A syllable in English has one vowel sound and 1-3 consonant sounds at the beginning or end.

> *book, re-**flect**, a-ca-**de**-mic*

word stress: the syllable in a word that is said more loudly and strongly

> *book, re-**flect**, a-ca-**de**-mic*

sentence stress: the words in a sentence that are said more loudly and strongly, usually content words (nouns, verbs, adjectives, adverbs)

> *I **stu**dy aca**de**mic **En**glish with Re**flect**.*

focus word: the most important word in a phrase or sentence; it usually provides new information and has the most stress. It is often the last word in a phrase or sentence.

> *I study **En**glish. I use a book called Re**flect**.*

intonation: the rise and fall of the voice (or pitch). Often our voice falls at the end of a sentence.

> *I **stu**dy aca**de**mic **En**glish with Re**flect**.*

USEFUL PHRASES FOR CLASSROOM COMMUNICATION

EXPRESS YOURSELF

Express opinions

I think...   In my opinion/view...
I believe...   Personally,...
I'm (not) sure...   To me,...

Express likes and dislikes

I like...   I hate...
I prefer...   I really don't like...
I love...   I don't care for...

Give facts

Studies show...
Researchers found...
The record shows...

Give tips or suggestions

You/We should/shouldn't/could...
You/We ought to...   It's (not) a good idea to...
Let's...   Why don't we/you...

Agree with someone

I agree. Absolutely.
True. Definitely
Good point. Right!
Exactly.

Disagree with someone

I disagree.
I'm not so sure about that.
I don't know.
That's a good point, but I don't agree.

PARTICIPATE IN CLASSROOM DISCUSSIONS

Check your understanding

So are you saying that...?
So what you mean is...?
What do you mean?
Do you mean...?
I'm not sure what you mean.

Ask for repetition

Could you say that again?
I'm sorry?
I didn't catch what you said.
I'm sorry. I missed that. What did you say?
Could you repeat that please?

Check others' understanding

Does that make sense?
Do you understand?
Is that clear?
Do you have any questions?

Ask for opinions

What do you think?
Do you have any thoughts?
What are your thoughts?
What's your opinion?

Take turns

Can/May I say something?
Could I add something?
Your turn.
You go ahead.

Interrupt politely

Excuse me.
Pardon me.
Forgive me for interrupting, but...
I hate to interrupt, but...

Make small talk

What do you do? (job)
Can you believe this weather?
How about this weather?
What do you do in your free time?
What do you do for fun?

Show interest

I see. Good for you.
Really? Seriously?
Um-hmm. No kidding!
Wow. And? (Then what?)
That's funny / amazing / incredible / awful!

Reflect is designed to provide practice for standardized exams, such as IELTS and TOEFL. This book has many activities that focus on and practice skills and question types that are needed for test success.

LISTENING • Key Skills	IELTS	TOEFL	Page(s)
Listen for causes and effects	x	x	23
Listen for gist or main ideas	x	x	7, 13, 23, 29, 38, 45, 55, 60, 71, 77, 87, 93, 102, 108, 119, 125
Listen for key details or examples	x	x	7, 13, 24, 29, 39, 45, 55, 60, 71, 75, 77, 87, 93, 103, 109, 119, 125
Listen for numbers or time words	x	x	40, 77, 102, 108
Predict what you might hear	x	x	7, 22, 38, 45, 54, 60, 71, 76, 102, 108, 119, 124
Recognize facts and opinions	x	x	87, 93
Take notes	x	x	45, 55, 108, 119

LISTENING • Common Question Types	IELTS	TOEFL	Page(s)
Check all the information that you hear		x	68, 101
Complete a paragraph or summary	x		63, 69, 78, 84, 101, 116
Complete a table, chart, notes, or map	x	x	4, 13, 23, 36, 40, 46, 55, 60, 62, 77, 94, 109, 110, 119, 126
Complete sentences	x		79, 87, 111
Match information to a category or person	x	x	29, 30, 60
Put information that you hear in order		x	45
Multiple choice	x	x	13, 23, 38, 39, 45, 77, 102, 125
Multiple response	x	x	7, 29, 55, 71, 87, 93, 119
Short answer	x		71, 109

SPEAKING • Key Skills	IELTS	TOEFL	Page(s)
Clarify or define words or ideas	x	x	47, 64
Evaluate information		x	46, 48
Express opinions about a topic	x	x	7, 24, 25, 35, 43, 53, 57, 69, 73, 74, 75, 89, 91, 96, 105, 117, 119
Give reasons or examples	x	x	24, 25, 57, 117, 119
Use questions	x	x	73, 80
Use signal words	x	x	127, 128

SPEAKING • Common Topics	IELTS	TOEFL	Page(s)
Art and design	x	x	53, 57, 58, 59, 64
Cities and neighborhoods	x	x	4, 5, 11, 27, 53
Games, sports, and entertainment	x		9, 123, 128
Goals, past and future plans	x	x	9, 16, 45, 74
Habits, daily activities, plans, and events	x	x	11, 45, 101, 106, 107, 109
Memories and past events	x	x	85, 89, 91, 96
News and current events	x		37, 40
Personal behavior and feelings	x	x	85, 89, 90, 101, 105, 121
Studying and learning	x	x	21, 25
Travel and tourism	x	x	68, 69, 80
Work, jobs, and skills	x	x	59
Yourself, your family, or other people	x		11, 20, 27, 43, 59, 73, 80, 90, 107, 123

CREDITS

Illustration: All illustrations are owned by © Cengage.

Cover © Trey Ratcliff; **2-3** (spread) Chang W Lee/The New York Times/Redux; **6** Richard Green/Alamy Stock Photo; **8** FG Trade/E+/Getty Images; **10** Sean Pavone/Alamy Stock Photo; **12** Lebrecht Music & Arts/Alamy Stock Photo; **14** Vanessal/Alamy Stock Photo; **18-19** (spread) Design Pics Inc/National Geographic Image Collection; **22** Jim Watson/AFP/Getty Images; **26** pidjoe/iStock/Getty Images; **27** Senryu/iStock/Getty Images; **28** © Chris Rainier for Enduring Voices Project; **29** Gary Blake/Alamy Stock Photo; **31** byakkaya/iStock/Getty Images; **34-35** (spread) Thomas Peschak/National Geographic Image Collection; **36** imageBroker/Alamy Stock Photo; **38** (br) pan demin/Shutterstock.com; **38-39** (spread) Stas Moroz/Shutterstock.com; **41** © Hammish Stubbs; **42** Universal History Archive/Universal Images Group/Getty Images; **43** Oakozhan/Alamy Stock Photo; **44-45** (spread) Paul Harris/Archive Photos/Getty Images; **46** Andia/Universal Images Group/Getty Images; **50-51** (spread) Philippe Lopez/AFP/Getty Images; **52-53** (spread) Jon Hicks/The Image Bank Unreleased/Getty Images; **54-56** Courtesy of Zul Zero; **58** (bl) NextMarsMedia/Shutterstock.com, (bc) Christopher Holt/Alamy Stock Photo, (br) Sina Vodjani/Alamy Stock Photo; **60-61** (spread) Fred R Conrad/The New York Times/Redux; **62** Nino Marcutti/Alamy Stock Photo; **66-67** (spread) Beverly Joubert/National Geographic Image Collection; **68** © Lee Narraway; **70** Alan Dawson/Alamy Stock Photo; **72** Keystone-France/Gamma-Keystone/Getty Images; **75** Ralph Lee Hopkins/National Geographic Image Collection; **76** Frans Lanting/National Geographic Image Collection; **78** Popperfoto/Getty Images; **82-83** (spread) © Maggie Steber; **85** Bloom image/Getty Images; **86** Thomas Barwick/DigitalVision/Getty Images; **91** David Pu'u/The Image Bank/Getty Images; **92** Rebecca Hale/National Geographic Image Collection; **98-99** (spread) Evgenia Arbugaeva/National Geographic Image Collection; **100** damircudic/E+/Getty Images; **102-103** (spread) Customdesigner/Shutterstock.com; **104** Dmitry Marchenko/Alamy Stock Photo; **106** Courtesy of Adnan Onart; **108-109** (spread) © Sebastian Wahlhuetter; **110** Nicola Katie/E+/Getty Images; **114-115** (spread) Jean Chung/Bloomberg/Getty Images; **117** Edward Wong/South China Morning Post/Getty Images; **118** Rebeca Figueiredo Amorim/Getty Images Sport/Getty Images; **121** adamkaz/E+/Getty Images; **124-125** (spread) Jeff Mauritzen/National Geographic Image Collection; **125-126** (b) © Internet for Elephants.